SYMPHONY THEMES

Arranged Alphabetically by Composer

SYMPHONY

Themes

compiled by

RAYMOND BURROWS

Assistant Professor of Music Education
Teachers College, Columbia University

BESSIE CARROLL REDMOND

Chairman of the Music Department
Benjamin Franklin High School
New York City

SIMON AND SCHUSTER

New York

Introduction

HEAVEN KNOWS, there are plenty of guides to music on the market. The number of "how" books must run into the hundreds—How to Listen to a Symphony, How to Analyze a Symphony, How to Read a Score, How to Enjoy a Symphony. I am sure there must be one on How to Dislike a Symphony. But so far as I know, until this book was printed, no one had thought of simply listing the main themes of the most played symphonies—saying, in effect, "Here's what they're made of" —and letting it go at that.

This book ought to be as useful to the expert as to the tyro. Ask me to quote the main theme of the first movement of the "*Eroica*," and I start off, bravely, "Ta, dee da-da, ta-da-dee tum-pa DA."

"Very good," you say. "And what happens then?"

And there you have me. I can quote you the charming passage where the clarinet, oboe, and flute build a little climax (it's number four in the analysis of the first movement on page 62); but meanwhile I have forgotten two other phrases that, short as they may be, are undeniably themes. It isn't that I am not reasonably familiar with the "*Eroica*." It is merely that, even among orchestral conductors, there are probably not three men in the world who could quote you, unprompted, *all* the themes of the one hundred symphonies that are herein analyzed. The great Toscanini might do it; but even he, I'll wager, would have to do a bit of homework first. So, as I say, even for the professional musician the book is valuable as a reference and a reminder.

For the layman it should prove a godsend. Most books dealing with symphonic form and analysis are either too technical, or too verbose, or both. "At this point in the exposition," the author rattles on, cheerfully, "a new theme enters, based on an inversion of the first three notes of the second subsidiary following the announcement of the main theme at bar 22. This is

5

developed in double counterpoint against a pedal E-flat in the basses and cellos—" whereupon the bewildered layman, convinced that there is something wrong with his brain, goes upstairs and quietly hangs himself.

Nor do the miniature scores help much. To a student of orchestration, or one who aspires to become an orchestral conductor, carrying a score to a concert and following the music through its pages is an invaluable part of his education. To the average music lover, who asks nothing more than to be able to recognize the themes and trace their progress, an attempt to follow the score involves chasing the themes through a jungle of notes and clefs that generally leaves him panting along, fifty bars behind the orchestra.

Here, on the other hand, is just what the listener wants to know, and all that he, lay or expert, *needs* to know: the stuff of which symphonies are made, the themes, set down in their pristine form, as the composer conceived them, without adornment or comment. If you can read notes (and if you can't learn, inside a week, to read notes, you had better emulate the layman I mentioned above), you will find in these pages just enough reading matter to keep you posted, and not so much as to prevent your hearing the music. Whether you sit before your radio, or before your phonograph, or in S-22, you will find them rewarding.

DEEMS TAYLOR

Foreword

SOPHISTICATED MUSICIANS, experienced concertgoers, amateur musicians, and just plain music lovers are daily listening to symphonies by radio and in the concert hall. What do they hear? How many really get the point? Can they recognize the important melodies of a symphony when they are first introduced and follow them through an entire movement?

Many academic helps have been devised for the understanding of the symphonies. Music history, musical form, the study of harmony, the analysis of the orchestra, and interpretative descriptions of the music have been of help to those who have had the time and energy to study them. The simple fact is, however, that the best way to understand what music is talking about is to have a simple statement of the subject itself. Most symphonic movements have two or more subjects which can be very quickly stated.

The authors found that students in high school and college have long needed a compilation of symphonic themes. While there is an educational value in developing the research technics of finding source materials, there are many times when students will have to manage without thematic references if they are obliged to search through huge scores or lengthy discussions for a few fragmentary music quotations. When the music is at hand, a book of themes, and themes alone, is a welcome asset.

It was a pleasant surprise to learn from amateur lovers of music that this type of reference was needed by them as well as by the music student. A little thought, however, made us realize that the themes themselves were the important thing, and that the same compilation which would serve a college class in symphonic appreciation could also be useful to concertgoers and radio listeners throughout the country.

In addition to listings of scores, recordings, and articles in books and magazines, the references include analytic program

7

notes. Careful study has been made to eliminate those program notes which merely mention the performance of a symphony and to include only those which give an analysis.

Some will make more use than others of the references listed herein, but it is hoped that all will profit from closer acquaintance with symphonic themes—upon which all symphonies are built.

The selection of the 100 symphonies most deserving of inclusion has not been easy. Several eminent authorities on symphonic music, including the music directors of two large broadcasting companies, were invited to recommend lists. The programs of major symphony orchestras over a period of years were studied for frequency of performance, and record catalogues were carefully scrutinized. The resultant list includes all symphonies that are frequently performed or readily available on records, and many of those which occasionally find their way into concert programs.

A natural interest in the development of American symphonic literature has prompted us to include some of the recent works by native composers, even though their frequency of performance does not yet rank with that of European masterpieces.

The naming of themes as principal, subordinate, episode, etc., has demonstrated such lack of uniformity among established symphonic analysts that we have simply stated the important themes of each movement and numbered them successively. The theme is given in the form in which it first appears except in those cases where the first entry is purely fragmentary.

In each case the theme has been stated in the simplest form which will give an accurate indication of its character. Harmonies and contrapuntal effects have been included only where they are essential to the theme itself. When the tempo mark is not repeated in successive themes in the same movement of a symphony, the same tempo given previously applies.

Foreign-language phrases which do not represent common musical terms have been translated into English. The definition of all musical terms used will be found in the glossary.

While every effort has been made to check and recheck the material for accuracy, it is inevitable that some errors must have found their way into a text of such complexity. The authors invite those who use this book to report any error discovered so that it may be corrected in future editions.

The authors are indebted to Richard Redmond for his vision of the musical importance of this book; to Richard L. Simon for his constant encouragement in the undertaking; to Vivienne Baum for assistance in collecting reference material; Douglas McKinnon of Radio Station WQXR; Alfred Wallenstein, conductor; and Robert A. Simon, music critic of *The New Yorker*, for advice in the selection of the 100 most important symphonies; to Wallace Brockway for editorial assistance; to Carleton Sprague Smith and his staff in the music division of the New York Public Library, especially Ella Poindexter; and to Paul Breisach and Myron Schaeffer for a careful and detailed criticism of the entire material.

RAYMOND BURROWS
BESSIE CARROLL REDMOND

Acknowledgments

Our thanks are due to:

AMERICAN MUSIC CENTER *for permission to quote from* Aaron Copland's Dance Symphony; ASSOCIATED MUSIC PUBLISHERS, INC., *for their permission to quote from* Mahler's Symphonies Nos. 2, 3, and 4; *from* Sibelius' Symphonies Nos. 1, 2, 4, 5, and 7; *from* Strauss' Alpine Symphony (Opus 64); RUSSELL BENNETT and his publishers, HARMS, INC., *for their permission to quote from* Abraham Lincoln Symphony, copyright, 1931, by Harms, Inc.; C. C. BIRCHARD & Co. *for their permission to quote from* Bloch's Symphony, "America"; Hanson's Symphony No. 2 in C major (Opus 30), Romantic, and Symphony No. 3 in A minor, and to the author for permission to quote these two symphonies as well as Symphony No. 1 in E minor (Opus 21); EDWARD BURLINGAME HILL *for his permission to quote from* Symphony No. 2 in C major and Symphony No. 3 in G major; ELKAN-VOGEL CO. INC., Philadelphia, and RONART LeROLLE *for permission to quote from* Chausson's Symphony in B♭ major (Opus 20); these publishers and MAURICE SENART, Paris, *for permission to quote from* Honegger's Symphony for Orchestra, copyright, 1930, by Elkan-Vogel Co.; these publishers and A. DURAND & SON, Paris, *for permission to quote from* d'Indy's Symphony No. 2 in B♭ major (Opus 57), and Saint-Saëns, Symphony No. 3, copyright, 1886, by Elkan-Vogel Co.; THE H. W. GRAY COMPANY and NOVELLO & Co. *for their permission to quote from* Elgar's Symphony No. 1 in A♭ major (Opus 55) and Symphony No. 2 in E♭ major (Opus 63); WILHELM HANSEN of Copenhagen *for permission to quote from* Sibelius' Symphony No. 6; ROY HARRIS *for his permission to quote from his* Symphonies Nos. 2 and 3; ROBERT LINEAU, Berlin-Lichterfelde, *for permission to quote from* Sibelius' Symphony No. 3; DANIEL GREGORY MASON *for his permission to quote from* Symphony No. 3 in B♭ major (Opus 35); MURDOCH, MURDOCH & Co. and CARL FISCHER, INC., *for their permission to quote from* Bax's Symphony No. 3; MUSIC DEPARTMENT OF THE OXFORD UNIVERSITY PRESS OF LONDON and RALPH VAUGHAN WILLIAMS *for their permission to quote from* Symphony in F minor; J. CURWEN & SONS, LTD., of London, *for their permission to quote from* Pastoral Symphony; and STAINER AND BELL, *for their permission to quote from* London Symphony; G. SCHIRMER, INC., *for their permission to quote from* Hadley's Symphony No. 4 in D minor; LEO SOWERBY *for permission to quote from his* Symphony No. 2; EDWIN J. STRINGHAM *for his permission to quote from* Symphony No. 1 in B♭ minor; CLAYTON F. SUMMY Co. and C. F. PETERS, Leipzig, *for their permission to quote from* Mahler's Symphony No. 5.

11

KEY TO CONTENTS

Table of Contents

A REFERENCE LIST OF SCORES, ANALYSES,
AND PROGRAM NOTES

References to program notes have been taken from those of the Chicago, Detriot, Minneapolis, Philadelphia, and New York Philharmonic orchestras. Only those having detailed analysis have been selected.

Numbers indicate seasons, as, Boston (season) 50; Minneapolis 6(3); sixth season, third concert.

L.S. = Large score   S.S. = Small score

M.S. = Miniature score

13

BEETHOVEN, LUDWIG VAN

Goetschius (*Analytic Series*), No. 21

Goetschius (*Masters of the Symphony*),
pp. 94–100

Grove (*Beethoven*), pp. 3–15

Murphy (*Symphonies of Beethoven*), v. 1

Newmarch (*Concert Goer's Library*), v. 4,
pp. 3–6

Tovey (*Essays in Analysis*), v. 1, pp. 22–25

Upton and Borowski (*Standard Concert
Guide*), pp. 28–32

PROGRAM NOTES Boston 15; 16; 20

Chicago 23

Detroit 6; 11

Minn. 13(2); 15(20); 21(3); 28(11)

Symphony No. 2 in D major (Opus 36)   60

L.S. Leipzig: Breitkopf & Härtel (1862)

Bonn: N. Simrock (1822)

Leipzig: C. F. Peters (1902)

S.S. Eulenberg Ed. No. 419; Kalmus Ed.
No. 2

M.S. New York: Harcourt, Brace & Co.
(1935)

ANALYSES Evans (*Beethoven*), v. 1, pp. 63–127

Goepp (*Symphonies*), v. 2, pp. 62–83

Goetschius (*Analytic Series*), No. 31

Goetschius (*Masters of the Symphony*),
pp. 100–05

Grove (*Beethoven*), pp. 23–42

Howes (*Musical Pilgrim*), v. 30, pp.
7–12

Murphy (*Symphonies of Beethoven*), v. 1

Newmarch (*Concert Goer's Library*), v. 4,
pp. 6–8

Tovey (*Essays in Analysis*), v. 1, pp. 25–29

Upton and Borowski (*Standard Concert
Guide*), pp. 32–37

PROGRAM NOTES Boston 9; 17; 19; 21

Detroit 7; 18

CONTENTS

BEETHOVEN, LUDWIG VAN

ANALYSES   Evans (*Beethoven*), v. 1, pp. 227–301
Goepp (*Symphonies*), v. 2, pp. 88–110
Goetschius (*Analytic Series*), No. 34
Goetschius (*Masters of the Symphony*),
    pp. 113–17
Grove (*Beethoven*), pp. 103–25
Murphy (*Symphonies of Beethoven*), v. 1
Newmarch (*Concert Goer's Library*), v. 1,
    pp. 8–11
Tovey (*Essays in Analysis*), v. 1, pp. 34–
    37
Tretbar (*Analytical Reviews*)
Upton & Borowski (*Standard Concert
    Guide*), pp. 41–45

PROGRAM NOTES   Boston 9; 16; 18; 20
Chicago 23
Detroit 7; 11; 16; 17
Minn. 7(4); 8(11); 21(5); 26(6)

✗Symphony No. 5 in C minor (Opus 67), "Fate"   66

L.S.   Leipzig: Breitkopf & Härtel (1862)
Mainz: B. Schott's Söhne (187–)
Leipzig: C. F. Peters (1872)
Cranz Edition (1924–25)

S.S.   Eulenberg Ed. No. 402; Kalmus Ed.
    No. 5

M.S.   New York: Harcourt, Brace & Co.
    (1935)

ANALYSES   Evans (*Beethoven*), v. 1, pp. 305–81
Goepp (*Symphonies*), v. 1, pp. 147–76
Goetschius (*Analytic Series*), No. 3
Goetschius (*Masters of the Symphony*),
    pp. 118–24
Grove (*Beethoven*), pp. 141–74
Murphy (*Symphonies of Beethoven*), v. 1
Newmarch (*Concert Goer's Library*), v. 4,
    pp. 8–11
Osborne (*Centuries of Progress in Music*),
    pp. 111–16
Porte (*Famous Symphonies*), pp. 6–10

CONTENTS

BEETHOVEN, LUDWIG VAN

M.S.	New York: Harcourt, Brace & Co. (1935)
ANALYSES	Evans (*Beethoven*), v. 2, pp. 93–176
	Goepp (*Symphonies*), v. 1, pp. 125–47
	Goetschius (*Analytic Series*), No. 26
	Goetschius (*Masters of the Symphony*), pp. 133–40
	Grove (*Beethoven*), pp. 241–67
	Murphy (*Symphonies of Beethoven*), v. 2
	Newmarch (*Concert Goer's Library*), v. 4, pp. 11–16
	Tovey (*Essays in Analysis*), v. 1, pp. 57–61
	Tretbar (*Analytical Reviews*)
	Upton & Borowski (*Standard Concert Guide*), pp. 52–56
PROGRAM NOTES	Boston 9; 15; 17; 19–21; 26; 28; 30
	Chicago 23
	Detroit 9; 11; 14; 15; 17
	Minn. 6(1); 13(3); 18(16); 19(7); 21(7); 25(5); 28(7); 29(2)
	Philadelphia 14

Symphony No. 8 in F major (Opus 93)   74

L.S.	Leipzig: Breitkopf & Härtel (1862)
	Vienna: S. A. Steiner (1816)
	Vienna: T. Haslinger (1837)
	Braunschweig: H. Litoff (1870)
	Leipzig: Peters Ed. (1902)
S.S.	Eulenberg Ed. No. 416; Kalmus Ed. No. 8
M.S.	New York: Harcourt, Brace & Co. (1935)
ANALYSES	Evans (*Beethoven*), v. 2, pp. 179–296
	Goepp (*Symphonies*), v. 2, pp. 111–32
	Goetschius (*Analytic Series*), No. 37
	Goetschius (*Masters of the Symphony*), pp. 140–46
	Grove (*Beethoven*), pp. 284–308
	Murphy (*Symphonies of Beethoven*), v. 2

CONTENTS

BEETHOVEN, LUDWIG VAN

Symphony No. 9 in D minor (Opus 125), "Choral" 76

19

BENNETT, ROBERT RUSSELL (1894–)
Abraham Lincoln Symphony 78

L.S.   Harms, Inc. (1931)
S.S.   None
ANALYSES   None
PROGRAM NOTES   Philadelphia 32

BERLIOZ, HECTOR (1803–1869)
Fantastic Symphony in C major (Opus 14) 80

L.S.   Brandus & Co. (185–)
S.S.   Eulenberg Ed. No. 422
ANALYSES   Elliot (*Berlioz*), pp. 121–26; 136–43
                Goepp (*Symphonies*), v. 2, pp. 457–62
                Mason (*Romantic Composers*), pp. 277–
                    80
                Osborne (*Centuries of Progress in Music*),
                    pp. 154–58
                Porte (*Famous Symphonies*), pp. 28–33
                Wotta (in *Musical Pilgrim*), v. 21, pp.
                    5–31
PROGRAM NOTES   Boston 17; 20; 24; 28; 37; 39; 42; 45
                Detroit 6
                Minn. 9(9); 20(15)
                Philadelphia 14

BLOCH, ERNEST (1880–)
Symphony "America" 82

L.S.   New York: C. C. Birchard & Co.
                    (1928)
M.S.   New York: C. C. Birchard & Co.
ANALYSES   Morgan (Bloch) (*Scottish Musical Mag-
                    azine*), v. 11, pp. 79–82
                Upton & Borowski (*Standard Concert
                    Guide*), pp. 93–96
PROGRAM NOTES   Boston 48
                Minn. 26(16); 27(7)
                Philadelphia 29
                Philharmonic 87

BORODIN, ALEXANDER (1834–1887)
Symphony No. 2 in B minor (Opus 5) 86

L.S.   Moscow: W. Bessel & Co. (188–)
                St. Petersburg: M. P. Belaieff (1889)

CONTENTS

BRAHMS, JOHANNES

PROGRAM NOTES   Boston 9; 15; 17; 19; 22; 24; 26–8; 30–
4; 36; 39

Detroit 7; 8; 13–15

Minn. 6(3); 7(5); 9(3); 10(10); 12(8);
13(8); 14(9); 15(11); 16(10); 17(8);
18(16); 19(12); 20(3); 21(15);
23(16); 25(1); 27(11); 29(7); 30(16);
31(10); 32(16); 34(7); 36(1)

Symphony No. 2 in D major (Opus 73)   92

L.S.   Berlin: N. Simrock (1878)

S.S.   Eulenberg Ed. No. 426; Kalmus Ed.
No. 14

M.S.   New York: Harcourt, Brace & Co.
(1935)

ANALYSES   Browne (*Musical Pilgrim*), v. 32, pp.
27–41

Evans (*Brahms*), 2nd ser. pp. 26–42

Goepp (*Symphonies*), v. 1, pp. 377–403

Goetschius (*Analytic Series*), No. 6

Goetschius (*Masters of the Symphony*),
pp. 234–38

Newmarch (*Concert Goer's Library*),
v. 1, pp. 19–22

Tovey (*Essays in Analysis*), v. 1, pp.
95–106

PROGRAM NOTES   Boston 15; 18; 19

Chicago 23

Detroit 6–8; 11; 15; 17; 18

Minn. 7; 9(8); 11(2); 13(14); 15(4);
16(9); 18(4); 19(9); 20(5); 23(1);
26(5); 28(6); 30(11); 32(11); 34(1);
35

Symphony No. 3 in F major (Opus 90)   94

L.S.   Berlin: N. Simrock (1886)

S.S.   Eulenberg Ed. No. 427; Kalmus Ed.
No. 15

M.S.   New York: Harcourt, Brace & Co.
(1935)

ANALYSES   Browne (*Musical Pilgrim*), v. 32, pp.
41–56

CONTENTS

23

BRAHMS, JOHANNES

BRUCKNER, ANTON (1824–1896)

Symphony No.4 in E♭ major (Op. 62), "Romantic"   100

Symphony No. 7 in E major (Opus 65)   102

CONTENTS

DVOŘÁK, ANTONÍN

      The Midland Musician, v. 2, pp. 43–49
PROGRAM NOTES Philharmonic 90; 97

**Symphony No. 5 in E minor (Opus 95),
"From the New World"**   112

L.S.   Berlin: N. Simrock (1894) (1903)
S.S.   Eulenberg Ed. No. 433; Kalmus Ed.
      No. 18
ANALYSES Goepp (*Symphonies*), v. 3, pp. 200–07
      Goetschius (*Analytic Series*), No. 9
      Goetschius (*Masters of the Symphony*),
       pp. 280–83
      Mason (*New Music Review*), v. 16, pp.
       682–86
      Mason (*Short Studies of Great Master-
       pieces*), pp. 126–39
      Newmarch (*Concert Goer's Library*),
       v. 1, pp. 23–25
      Osborne (*Centuries of Progress in Music*),
       pp. 301–08
      Porte (*Famous Symphonies*), pp. 72–76
      Tovey (*Essays in Analysis*), v. 2, pp.
       106–10
PROGRAM NOTES Boston 16; 17; 20; 24; 28; 30; 32; 37;
      39
      Chicago 23
      Detroit 7; 17
      Minn. 6(6); 9(6); 12(10); 17(9);
       18(12); 20(8); 22(1); 25(2); 28
      Philadelphia 14

ELGAR, EDWARD (1857–1934)
Symphony No. 1 in A♭ major (Opus 55), "English" 114

L.S.   London: Novello & Co., Ltd. (1908)
S.S.   None
ANALYSES Goepp (*Symphonies*), v. 3, pp. 308–20
      Grove (*Musical Times*), v. 49, pp. 778–
       80
      Maine (*Elgar*), pp. 124–55
      Mason (*Contemporary Composers*), pp.
       122–32

CONTENTS

27

FRANCK, CESAR

Goetschius (*Analytic Series*), No. 10

Goetschius (*Masters of the Symphony*), pp. 303–06

Mason (*New Music Review*), v. 16, pp. 502–05

Mason (*Short Studies of Great Master-pieces*), pp. 60–71

Newmarch (*Concert Goer's Library*), v. 1, pp. 35–38

O'Connell (*Victor Book of the Symphony*), pp. 203–07

Osborne (*Centuries of Progress in Music*), pp. 255–62

Porte (*Famous Symphonies*), pp. 90–93

Tovey (*Essays in Analysis*), v. 2, pp. 62–69

Upton & Borowski (*Standard Concert Guide*), pp. 190, 191

PROGRAM NOTES   Boston 18; 19; 24; 29; 31; 33; 34; 36; 38

Chicago 23

Detroit 6; 8; 11; 14

Minn. 6(7); 7(9); 9(12); 11(6); 15(7); 16(5); 18(8); 20(2); 22(9); 23(12); 24(11); 30(11); 31(6); 34(16)

Philadelphia 12; 14; 16; 17; 21

Philharmonic 76

GLAZUNOV, ALEXANDER CONSTANTINOVICH (1865–)

Symphony No. 5 in B♭ major (Opus 55)   120

L.S.   Leipzig: M. P. Belaieff (1898)

S.S.   None

ANALYSES   Colles (*Oxford History of Music*), v. 7, pp. 247–54

Goetschius (*Masters of the Symphony*), p. 348

PROGRAM NOTES   Boston 26; 33

GOLDMARK, KARL (1830–1915)

Symphony in E♭ major (Opus 26), Rustic Wedding   122

L.S.   Mainz: B. Schott's Sons (1876)

CONTENTS

HARRIS, ROY (1898–)
Symphony No. 2   130

L.S.	None
S.S.	None
ANALYSES	None
PROGRAM NOTES	None

Symphony No. 3   131

L.S.	None
S.S.	None
ANALYSES	None
PROGRAM NOTES	Boston 58

HAYDN, JOSEPH (1732–1809)
Symphony No. 1 in E♭ major (B & H 103), "Drum-Roll"   132

L.S.	Leipzig: Breitkopf & Härtel (1854–67)
	Leipzig: Andre (1868–69)
	Leipzig: C. F. Peters (1873–74)
S.S.	Eulenberg Ed. No. 469
M.S.	New York: Harcourt, Brace & Co. (1936)
ANALYSES	Goepp (*Symphonies*), v. 1, pp. 55–67
	Tovey (*Essays in Analysis*), v. 1, pp. 170–73
	Upton & Borowski (*Standard Concert Guide*), pp. 264–66
	Upton (*Standard Symphonies*), pp. 152–55
PROGRAM NOTES	Boston 24; 30; 35
	Detroit 6
	Philadelphia 32

Symphony No. 2 in D major (B & H 104), "London"   134

L.S.	Leipzig: Breitkopf & Härtel (1854–67)
	Leipzig: C. F. Peters (1873–74)
S.S.	Eulenberg Ed. No. 409; Kalmus Ed. No. 24
M.S.	New York: Harcourt, Brace & Co. (1936)
ANALYSES	Fox (*Musical Pilgrim*), v. 20, pp. 10–17

CONTENTS

HAYDN, JOSEPH

Symphony No. 3 in E♭ major (B & H 99) (London No. 10)   136

Symphony No. 4 in D major (B & H 101), "Clock"   138

31

HAYDN, JOSEPH
Symphony No. 5 in D major (B & H 93) (London No. 2)   140

L.S.	Leipzig: Breitkopf & Härtel (1854–67)
S.S.	Eulenberg Ed. No. 468
ANALYSES	None
PROGRAM NOTES	Boston 20
	Minn. 29(2)
	Philharmonic 90

Symphony No. 6 in G major (B & H 94), "Surprise"   142

L.S.	Leipzig: Breitkopf & Härtel (1854–67)
S.S.	Eulenberg Ed. No. 435; Kalmus Ed. No. 25
ANALYSES	Goetschius (*Analytic Series*), No. 1
	Newmarch (*Concert Goer's Library*), v. 1, pp. 40–42
	O'Connell (*Victor Book of the Symphony*), pp. 235–37
	Osborne (*Centuries of Progress in Music*), pp. 71–77
	Tovey (*Essays in Analysis*), v. 1, pp. 147, 148
	Upton & Borowski (*Standard Concert Guide*), pp. 267–69
	Upton (*Standard Symphonies*), pp. 157–58
PROGRAM NOTES	Boston 15; 20; 27; 32; 34; 42; 45; 48
	Detroit 18
	Minn. 15(9); 21(2); 31(11)

Symphony No. 7 in C major (B & H 97) (London No. 1)   144

L.S.	Leipzig: Breitkopf & Härtel (1854–67)
S.S.	Eulenberg Ed. No. 483
M.S.	New York: Harcourt, Brace & Co. (1936)
ANALYSES	Haggin (*Symphonies*), pp. 45–49
	Newmarch (*Concert Goer's Library*), v. 4, pp. 38, 39
	O'Connell (*Victor Book of Symphonies*), pp. 237–38

CONTENTS

HAYDN, JOSEPH

M.S. New York: Harcourt, Brace & Co. (1936)

ANALYSES Goetschius (*Analytic Series*), No. 19

Tovey (*Essays in Analysis*), v. 1, pp. 159–62

Upton & Borowski (*Standard Concert Guide*), pp. 271, 272

Upton (*Standard Symphonies*), pp. 161–63

PROGRAM NOTES Boston 19
Detroit 13
Philadelphia 11; 14

Symphony No. 12 in B♭ major (B & H 102) (London No. 9) 152

L.S. Leipzig: Breitkopf & Härtel (1854–67)
S.S. Eulenberg Ed. No. 438
M.S. New York: Harcourt, Brace & Co. (1936)

ANALYSES Fox (*Musical Pilgrim*), v. 20, pp. 17–22

Goetschius (*Masters of the Symphony*), pp. 58–63

Tovey (*Essays in Analysis*), v. 1, pp. 164–70

Upton & Borowski (*Standard Concert Guide*), pp. 273, 274

Upton (*Standard Symphonies*), pp. 163–65

PROGRAM NOTES Boston 28; 33
Detroit 10; 14; 16

Symphony No. 45 in F♯ minor (B & H 18), "Farewell" 154

L.S. Offenbach am Main: J. Andre (1886)
S.S. Eulenberg Ed. No. 486
ANALYSES Goetschius (*Masters of the Symphony*), pp. 53–56
PROGRAM NOTES Philadelphia 26 (for reference only)

HILL, EDWARD BURLINGAME (1872–)

Symphony No. 2 in C major (Opus 35) 156

SCORE Unpublished
ANALYSES None

CONTENTS

MAHLER, GUSTAV

ANALYSES	Stefan (*Mahler*), pp. 101–03
PROGRAM NOTES	Philharmonic 80

Symphony No. 4 in G major   167

L.S.	Vienna: J. Weinberger, Universal Ed. (1904–09) Vienna: L. Doblinger
S.S.	None
ANALYSES	Stefan (*Mahler*), pp. 103–06 Upton & Borowski (*Standard Concert Guide*), pp. 325, 326
PROGRAM NOTES	Minn. 19(4); 35 Philharmonic 74

Symphony No. 5 in C♯ minor, "Giant"   170

L.S.	Leipzig: C. F. Peters (1904)
S.S.	None
ANALYSES	Goepp (*Symphonies*), v. 3, pp. 244–60 Stefan (*Mahler*), pp. 107, 108
PROGRAM NOTES	Philharmonic 85; 86; 90

MASON, DANIEL GREGORY (1873–)

Symphony No. 3 in B♭ major (Opus 35), "Lincoln"   174

L.S.	New York: Original manuscript (1937)
S.S.	None
ANALYSES	Downes (*New York Times*), Nov. 18, 1937
PROGRAM NOTES	Philharmonic 96

MENDELSSOHN-BARTHOLDY, FELIX (1809–1847)

Symphony No. 3 in A minor (Opus 56), "Scotch" 176

L.S.	Leipzig: Breitkopf & Härtel (1912) Leipzig: C. F. Peters (1876)
S.S.	Eulenberg Ed. No. 406
ANALYSES	Goepp (*Symphonies*), v. 2, pp. 230–41 Goetschius (*Analytic Series*), No. 8 Goetschius (*Masters of the Symphony*), pp. 194–200 Goodrich (*Complete Musical Analysis*), pp. 263–68

CONTENTS

MOZART, WOLFGANG AMADEUS

	Leipzig: Breitkopf & Härtel (1877–87)
S.S.	None
ANALYSES	Goetschius (*Masters of the Symphony*), pp. 66, 67
PROGRAM NOTES	None

Symphony No. 12 in G major (K 110)   184

L.S.	Leipzig: Breitkopf & Härtel (1877–87)
S.S.	None
ANALYSES	Goetschius (*Masters of the Symphony*), pp. 68–70
PROGRAM NOTES	None

Symphony No. 35 in D major (K 385), "Haffner" 186

L.S.	Leipzig: Breitkopf & Härtel (1877–87)
S.S.	Eulenberg Ed. No. 437
ANALYSES	Goetschius (*Analytic Series*), No. 23
	Goetschius (*Masters of the Symphony*), pp. 70–72
	Newmarch (*Concert Goer's Library*), v. 1, pp. 42, 43
PROGRAM NOTES	Boston 58 (for reference only)

Symphony No. 36 in C major (K 425), "Linz"   188

L.S.	Leipzig: Breitkopf & Härtel (1877–87)
S.S.	Eulenberg Ed. No. 502
M.S.	New York: Harcourt, Brace & Co. (1936)
ANALYSES	Tovey (*Essays in Analysis*), v. 1, pp. 183–86
PROGRAM NOTES	Boston 40
	Chicago 23
	Philharmonic 90

Symphony No. 37 in G major (K 444)   190

L.S.	Leipzig: Breitkopf & Härtel (1877–87)
S.S.	None
ANALYSES	None
PROGRAM NOTES	None

Symphony No. 38 in D major (K 504), "Prague— Without Minuet"   192

L.S.	Leipzig: Breitkopf & Härtel (1877–87)
S.S.	Eulenberg Ed. No. 446

CONTENTS

MOZART, WOLFGANG AMADEUS

Symphony No. 41 in C major (K 551), "Jupiter" 200

CONTENTS

SAINT-SAËNS, CHARLES CAMILLE

ANALYSES Goetschius (*Analytic Series*), No. 28

Goetschius (*Masters of the Symphony*), pp. 309–12

Hale (*Boston Sym. Program Notes*), pp. 255–58

Hervey (*Saint-Saëns*), pp. 98–101

Lyle (*Saint-Saëns*), pp. 110–14

Mason (*New Music Review*), v. 16, pp. 646–50

Mason (*Short Studies of Great Masterpieces*), pp. 114–25

Upton (*Standard Symphonies*), pp. 228–30

Upton & Borowski (*Standard Concert Guide*), pp. 411–12

PROGRAM NOTES Boston 20; 33; 37; 38; 42; 45; 47; 49; 57

Detroit 17

Minn. 11(7); 25(9)

Philadelphia 12

Philharmonic 86; 89

SCHUBERT, FRANZ (1808–1818)

Symphony No. 4 in C minor, "Tragic" **208**

L.S. Leipzig: Peters Ed. (1816)

Leipzig: Breitkopf & Härtel (1884–57)

S.S. Eulenberg Ed. No. 507

ANALYSES Goetschius (*Masters of the Symphony*), pp. 164–66

PROGRAM NOTES Philharmonic 93

Symphony No. 5 in B♭ major **210**

L.S. Leipzig: Breitkopf & Härtel (1884–1857)

S.S. Eulenberg Ed. No. 508

ANALYSES Goetschius (*Analytic Series*), No. 14

Goetschius (*Masters of the Symphony*), pp. 166–70

Tovey (*Essays in Analysis*), v. 1, pp. 203–05

PROGRAM NOTES Boston 48

Philharmonic 93

CONTENTS

SCHUBERT, FRANZ

O'Connell (*Victor Book of the Symphony*), pp. 352–54
Osborne (*Centuries of Progress in Music*), pp. 150–53
Porte (*Famous Symphonies*), pp. 127–30
Smith (*Musical Pilgrim*), v. 15, pp. 30–48
Tovey (*Essays in Analysis*), v. 1, pp. 211–15
Tretbar (*Analytical Reviews*)
Upton & Borowski (*Standard Concert Guide*), pp. 424, 425

PROGRAM NOTES Boston 9; 15–17; 19; 23; 25; 26; 28; 31; 33; 36; 38; 39
Detroit 7; 9; 13
Minn. 23(2); 25(3)

SCHUMANN, ROBERT ALEXANDER
(1810–1856)

Symphony No. 1 in B♭ major (Opus 38), "Spring" 216

L.S. Leipzig: Breitkopf & Härtel (1881–1893)
Leipzig: C. F. Peters (1888)
London: E. Donajonski (189–)
S.S. Eulenberg Ed. No. 417
M.S.

ANALYSES Goepp (*Symphonies*), v. 2, pp. 195–209
Goetschius (*Analytic Series*), No. 5, 17
Goetschius (*Masters of the Symphony*), pp. 207–11
Grove (*Musical Times*), v. 49, pp. 384–87
Hale (*Boston Symphony Program Notes*), pp. 274, 275
O'Connell (*Victor Book of the Symphony*), pp. 359–61
Prout (*Monthly Musical Record*), v. 2, pp. 30–33
Tovey (*Essays in Analysis*), v. 2, pp. 48–52
Tretbar (*Analytical Reviews*)

44

CONTENTS

SCHUMANN, ROBERT ALEXANDER

ANALYSES   Goepp (*Symphonies*), v. 1, pp. 314–41
Goetschius (*Analytic Series*), No. 32
Goetschius (*Masters of the Symphony*), pp. 219–23
Grove (*Musical Times*), v. 50, pp. 789–92
Hale (*Boston Symphony Program Notes*), pp. 278–81
O'Connell (*Victor Book of the Symphony*), pp. 364–66
Prout (*Monthly Musical Record*), v. 2, pp. 77–81
Tovey (*Essays in Analysis*), v. 2, pp. 53–56
Upton (*Standard Symphonies*), pp. 248–50
Upton & Borowski (*Standard Concert Guide*), pp. 436–37

PROGRAM NOTES   Boston 9; 16; 18; 20; 22; 24; 30; 36; 39; 42; 48; 51
Detroit 9
Minn. 33; 35
Philharmonic 89; 90; 94

Symphony No. 4 in D minor (Opus 120)   222

L.S.   Leipzig: Breitkopf & Härtel (1881–93)
Leipzig: C. F. Peters (1888)

S.S.   Eulenberg Ed. No. 413
Leipzig: Breitkopf & Härtel (1853)
Leipzig: Breitkopf & Härtel (1885)

ANALYSES   Goepp (*Symphonies*), v. 2, pp. 210–29
Goetschius (*Analytic Series*), No. 35
Goetschius (*Masters of the Symphony*), pp. 211–14
Hale (*Boston Symphony Program Notes*), pp. 284–85
O'Connell (*Victor Book of the Symphony*), pp. 367–69
Prout (*Monthly Musical Record*), v. 2, pp. 46–49
Tretbar (*Analytical Reviews*)

CONTENTS

SIBELIUS, JEAN
Symphony No. 2 in D major (Opus 43)   228

L.S.   Leipzig: Breitkopf & Härtel (1903)
S.S.   Leipzig: Breitkopf & Härtel (1903)
ANALYSES   Goddard (*Music and Letters*), v. 12,
                    pp. 156–63
                  Gray (*Musical Pilgrim*), v. 35, pp. 16–
                    26
                  Gray (*Sibelius*), pp. 134–37
                  Hale (*Boston Symphony Program Notes*),
                    pp. 295–97
                  O'Connell (*Victor Book of the Symphony*),
                    pp. 379–81
PROGRAM NOTES   Boston 23; 29; 30; 35; 41; 43; 49; 51–
                    3; 55; 57; 58
                  Detroit 7; 15
                  Minn. 30(4); 34(14); 36
                  Philharmonic 75

Symphony No. 3 in C major (Opus 52)   230

L.S.   Berlin: Schlesinger (1907)
S.S.   New York: E. F. Kalmus, Inc. (19__)
ANALYSES   Goetschius (*Masters of the Symphony*),
                    pp. 287–89
                  Gray (*Musical Pilgrim*), v. 35, pp. 27–
                    34
                  Gray (*Sibelius*), p. 137
                  Tovey (*Essays in Analysis*), v. 2, pp.
                    121–25
PROGRAM NOTES   Boston 48 (for reference only)

Symphony No. 4 in A minor (Opus 63)   232

L.S.   Leipzig: Breitkopf & Härtel (1912)
S.S.   Leipzig: Breitkopf & Härtel (1912)
ANALYSES   Downes (*Symphonic Masterpieces*), pp.
                    298–99
                  Gray (*Musical Pilgrim*), v. 35, pp. 34–
                    45
                  Gray (*Sibelius*), pp. 140–44
                  O'Connell (*Victor Book of the Symphony*),
                    pp. 382–84

48

CONTENTS

STRAUSS, RICHARD (1864)
Alpine Symphony (Opus 64)   241

L.S.   Leipzig: F. E. C. Leuckart (1915)
S.S.   Eulenberg Ed. No. 499
ANALYSES   Abell (*Musical Courier*), v. 71, No. 23, pp. 5–7
Finck (*Strauss*), pp. 212–18
Upton & Borowski (*Standard Concert Guide*), pp. 465, 466
PROGRAM NOTES   Boston 45; 49
Minn. 14(6)
Philadelphia 16
Philharmonic 75; 89

Symphony, Aus Italien (Opus 16)   244

L.S.   Munich: J. Aibl (1904)
S.S.   Eulenberg Ed. No. 478
ANALYSES   Donald (*Metronome*), v. 31, No. 1, pp. 42, 43
Finch (*Strauss*), pp. 152–54
PROGRAM NOTES   Boston 34

STRINGHAM, EDWIN (1890–)
Symphony No. 1 in B♭ minor   246

SCORE   None
ANALYSES   None
PROGRAM NOTES   Minn. 27(4)

TCHAIKOVSKY, PIOTR ILYICH (1840–1893)
Symphony No. 3 in D major (Opus 29), "Polish"   248

L.S.   Moscow: P. Jurgenson (1875)
S.S.   None
ANALYSES   Lee (*Tchaikovsky*), pp. 10–14
PROGRAM NOTES   Philharmonic 95

Symphony No. 4 in F minor (Opus 36)   250

L.S.   Leipzig: D. Rahter (1880)
S.S.   Eulenberg Ed. No. 430; Kalmus Ed. No. 58
ANALYSES   Blom (*Musical Pilgrim*), v. 25, pp. 23–42
Goepp (*Symphonies*), v. 3, pp. 116–25

CONTENTS

TCHAIKOVSKY, PIOTR ILYICH

✗ Symphony No. 5 in E minor (Opus 64)   252

TCHAIKOVSKY, PIOTR ILYICH
Philadelphia 14
Philharmonic 71; 72; 74–78

✕ Symphony No. 6 in B minor (Opus 74)
"Pathétique"   254

L.S. Moscow: P. Jurgenson (1894)
      Leipzig: R. Forberg (1906)
S.S. Eulenberg Ed. No. 479; Kalmus Ed.
      No. 60
ANALYSES Donald (*Metronome*), v. 34, No. 8, pp.
      43, 60, 61
      Goepp (*Symphonies*), v. 2, pp. 423–33
      Goetschius (*Analytic Series*), No. 7
      Goetschius (*Masters of the Symphony*),
      pp. 275–77
      Lee (*Tchaikovsky*), pp. 27–31
      Mason (*New Music Review*), v. 16, pp.
      574–78
      Mason (*Short Studies of Great Master-
      pieces*), pp. 85–98
      Newmarch (*Tchaikovsky*), pp. 307–59
      O'Connell (*Victor Book of the Symphony*),
      pp. 472–75
      Osborne (*Centuries of Progress in Music*),
      pp. 294–99
      Tovey (*Essays in Analysis*), v. 2, pp.
      184–89
      Upton & Borowski (*Standard Concert
      Guide*), pp. 492, 493
PROGRAM NOTES Boston 15–18
      Detroit 8; 9; 11; 14; 15; 17
      Minn. 6(2); 7(6); 9(11); 10 Carnegie;
      16(7); 19(8); 20(1); 22(6); 24(2);
      26(8); 28(16); 31(4); 34(15)

VAUGHAN WILLIAMS, RALPH
London Symphony   256
L.S. London: Stainer & Bell, Ltd. (1920)
S.S. London: Stainer & Bell, Ltd. (1920)
ANALYSES Dickenson (*Musical Pilgrim*), v. 18, pp.
      32–51

CONTENTS

Key to Instrument Abbreviations

B. Cl.	*Bass clarinet*		Ob.	*Oboe*
Br.	*Brass*		Organ	*Organ*
Bsn.	*Bassoon*		Piano	*Piano*
C. B.	*Contra bass*		Str.	*Strings*
C. Bsn.	*Contra bassoon*		Tr.	*Trumpet*
Cel	*Celesta*		Trbn.	*Trombone*
E. Hn.	*English horn*		Tu.	*Tuba*
Fl.	*Flute*		V.	*Violin*
F. O.	*Full orchestra*		Va.	*Viola*
Harp	*Harp*		Vc.	*Violoncello*
Hn.	*Horn*		W. W.	*Wood winds*
K. D.	*Kettledrums*		Xyl.	*Xylophone*

SYMPHONY THEMES

Arranged Alphabetically by Composer

BAX

Symphony No. 3, C major

FIRST MOVEMENT

SECOND MOVEMENT

THIRD MOVEMENT

BEETHOVEN

Symphony No. 1, C major, OP. 21 *1800*

FIRST MOVEMENT

SECOND MOVEMENT

3

THIRD MOVEMENT

1

2

FOURTH MOVEMENT

1

2

3

BEETHOVEN
Symphony No. 2, D major, op. 36 *1802*

FIRST MOVEMENT

SECOND MOVEMENT

THIRD MOVEMENT

FOURTH MOVEMENT

BEETHOVEN

Symphony No. 3, Eb major, op. 55 *1804*

"EROICA"

FIRST MOVEMENT

SECOND MOVEMENT

THIRD MOVEMENT Scherzo

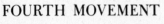

FOURTH MOVEMENT

BEETHOVEN

Symphony No. 4, Bb major, op. 60 *1806*

FIRST MOVEMENT

SECOND MOVEMENT

THIRD MOVEMENT

FOURTH MOVEMENT

BEETHOVEN

Symphony No. 5, C minor, op. 67

"FATE"

FIRST MOVEMENT

SECOND MOVEMENT

THIRD MOVEMENT

FOURTH MOVEMENT

BEETHOVEN

Symphony No. 6, F major, op. 68 1808

"PASTORAL"

FIRST MOVEMENT (Cheerful impressions received on arriving in the country)

SECOND MOVEMENT (By the brook)

THIRD MOVEMENT (Peasants' merry-making)

FOURTH MOVEMENT (Tempest and storm)

[concluded on next page]

BEETHOVEN
Symphony No. 6, F major, [concluded]

FIFTH MOVEMENT (The Shepherds Hymn - Thanksgiving after the storm)

BEETHOVEN

Symphony No. 7, A major, op. 92

FIRST MOVEMENT

SECOND MOVEMENT

3

THIRD MOVEMENT

1

2

FOURTH MOVEMENT

1

2

3

4

BEETHOVEN

Symphony No. 8, F major, OP. 93 *1812*

FIRST MOVEMENT

SECOND MOVEMENT

THIRD MOVEMENT

FOURTH MOVEMENT

BEETHOVEN
Symphony No. 9, D minor, op. 125 *1817–23*
"CHORAL"

FIRST MOVEMENT

SECOND MOVEMENT

THIRD MOVEMENT

FOURTH MOVEMENT

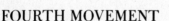

BENNETT

Abraham Lincoln, 1929

FIRST MOVEMENT His simplicity and his sadness

SECOND MOVEMENT His affection and his faith

THIRD MOVEMENT His humor and his weakness

FOURTH MOVEMENT His greatness and his sacrifice

BERLIOZ

Fantastic Symphony, C major, OP. 14 *1831*

FIRST MOVEMENT Reveries- Passions

SECOND MOVEMENT A Ball

THIRD MOVEMENT Scenes in the Country

FOURTH MOVEMENT March to the Gallows

FIFTH MOVEMENT Dance of a Witches' Sabbath

BLOCH

America, G minor *1928*

FIRST MOVEMENT The Soil

The Call of America — Moderato (♩=94)

Old Chanty — Più moderato (♩=88)

Land in Sight

America — Giocoso-marcato molto

Memories of the Past — Poco animato (♩=96)

Building up a Nation — A tempo (♩=66) poco lento

Old Hundred — Poco più sostenuto (♩=69)

[concluded on next pages]

BLOCH

America, G minor *1928* [continued]

SECOND MOVEMENT 1861 - 1865

THIRD MOVEMENT 1926 The Present and the Future

BORODIN

Symphony No. 2, B minor, op. 5 1871–7

FIRST MOVEMENT

SECOND MOVEMENT

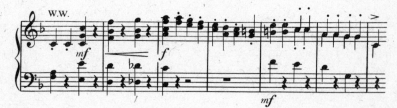

3

THIRD MOVEMENT

1

2

3

FOURTH MOVEMENT

1

2

BRAHMS

Symphony No. 1, C minor, op. 68 *1876*

FIRST MOVEMENT

SECOND MOVEMENT

THIRD MOVEMENT

[concluded on next pages]

BRAHMS

Symphony No. 1, C minor, [continued]

FOURTH MOVEMENT

BRAHMS

Symphony No. 2, D major, OP. 73 1877

FIRST MOVEMENT

SECOND MOVEMENT

THIRD MOVEMENT

FOURTH MOVEMENT

BRAHMS

Symphony No. 3, F major, op. 90

FIRST MOVEMENT

SECOND MOVEMENT

THIRD MOVEMENT

FOURTH MOVEMENT

BRAHMS

Symphony No. 4, E minor, op. 98 1885

FIRST MOVEMENT

SECOND MOVEMENT

[concluded on next pages]

BRAHMS

Symphony No. 4, E minor, [continued]

THIRD MOVEMENT

FOURTH MOVEMENT

Variation 4 {

BRUCKNER

Symphony No. 4, Eb major, op. 62 *1880*

"ROMANTIC"

FIRST MOVEMENT

SECOND MOVEMENT

THIRD MOVEMENT Scherzo

FOURTH MOVEMENT

BRUCKNER

Symphony No. 7, E major, op. 65 *1881—*

FIRST MOVEMENT

SECOND MOVEMENT

THIRD MOVEMENT Scherzo

FOURTH MOVEMENT

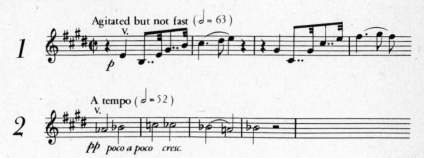

BRUCKNER

Symphony No. 9, D minor, op. 67 *1891–4*

"YOUTH"

FIRST MOVEMENT

SECOND MOVEMENT (Scherzo)

THIRD MOVEMENT

CHAUSSON

Symphony, Bb major, op. 20 *1890*

FIRST MOVEMENT

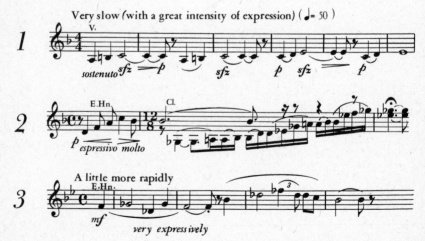

SECOND MOVEMENT

THIRD MOVEMENT

COPLAND

Dance Symphony, 1922–5

FIRST MOVEMENT

SECOND MOVEMENT

THIRD MOVEMENT

DVOŘÁK

Symphony No. 4, G major, op. 88 *1889*

FIRST MOVEMENT

SECOND MOVEMENT

3

THIRD MOVEMENT

1

2

FOURTH MOVEMENT

Introductory

1

DVOŘÁK

Symphony No. 5, E minor, op. 95 *1893*

"FROM THE NEW WORLD"

FIRST MOVEMENT

SECOND MOVEMENT

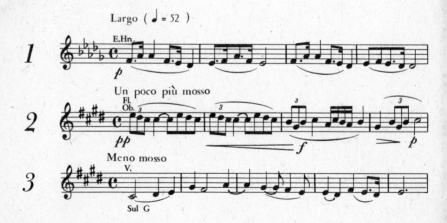

THIRD MOVEMENT Scherzo

ELGAR

Symphony No. 1, A♭ major, OP. 55 *1908*

"ENGLISH"

FIRST MOVEMENT

SECOND MOVEMENT Scherzo

THIRD MOVEMENT

FOURTH MOVEMENT

ELGAR

Symphony No. 2, Eb major, op. 63 *1911*

"MEMORIAL TO KING EDWARD"

FIRST MOVEMENT

SECOND MOVEMENT

THIRD MOVEMENT   Rondo

FOURTH MOVEMENT

FRANCK

Symphony in D minor *1886–8*

FIRST MOVEMENT

SECOND MOVEMENT

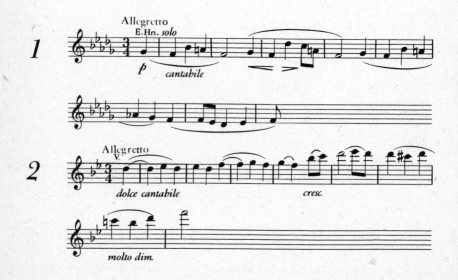

3

THIRD MOVEMENT

1

2

GLAZUNOV

Symphony No. 5, Bb major, OP. 55 *1897*

FIRST MOVEMENT

SECOND MOVEMENT Scherzo

THIRD MOVEMENT

FOURTH MOVEMENT

GOLDMARK

Rustic Wedding Symphony,

Eb major, OP. 26 *1896*

FIRST MOVEMENT Wedding March Variations

SECOND MOVEMENT Bridal Song

THIRD MOVEMENT Serenade

FOURTH MOVEMENT In the Garden

FIFTH MOVEMENT Dance

HADLEY

Symphony No. 4, D minor, op. 64 *1911*

"NORTH, EAST, SOUTH, WEST"

FIRST MOVEMENT North

SECOND MOVEMENT East

THIRD MOVEMENT South (Scherzo)

FOURTH MOVEMENT West

HANSON
Symphony No. 1, E minor, OP. 21 *1922*
"NORDIC"

FIRST MOVEMENT To Felix Lamond

SECOND MOVEMENT To my Mother

THIRD MOVEMENT To my Father

HANSON
Symphony No. 2, C major, op. 30 *1930*
"ROMANTIC"

FIRST MOVEMENT

SECOND MOVEMENT

THIRD MOVEMENT

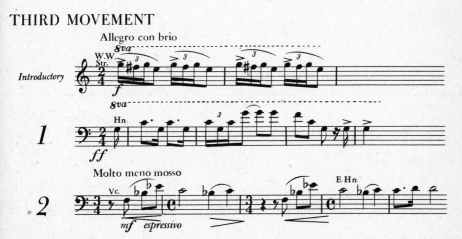

HANSON

Symphony No. 3, A minor, *1937*

FIRST MOVEMENT

SECOND MOVEMENT

THIRD MOVEMENT

FOURTH MOVEMENT

HARRIS
Symphony No. 2

FIRST MOVEMENT

SECOND MOVEMENT

THIRD MOVEMENT

HARRIS
Symphony No. 3

IN ONE MOVEMENT

HAYDN

Symphony No. 1, Eb major, B & H 103 1795

"DRUM ROLL"

FIRST MOVEMENT

SECOND MOVEMENT

THIRD MOVEMENT

FOURTH MOVEMENT

HAYDN

Symphony No. 2, D major, B & H 104 *179*

"LONDON"

FIRST MOVEMENT

SECOND MOVEMENT

THIRD MOVEMENT (Menuetto)

FOURTH MOVEMENT

HAYDN

Symphony No. 3, Eb major, B & H 99 *1793*

"LONDON NO. 10"

FIRST MOVEMENT

SECOND MOVEMENT

THIRD MOVEMENT Menuetto

FOURTH MOVEMENT

HAYDN

Symphony No. 4, D major, B & H 101 1794

"CLOCK"

FIRST MOVEMENT

SECOND MOVEMENT

THIRD MOVEMENT Menuetto

FOURTH MOVEMENT

HAYDN

Symphony No. 5, D major, B & H 93 1791

"LONDON NO. 2"

FIRST MOVEMENT

SECOND MOVEMENT

THIRD MOVEMENT (Menuetto)

2

FOURTH MOVEMENT

2

HAYDN

Symphony No. 6, G major, B & H 94 1792

"SURPRISE"

FIRST MOVEMENT

SECOND MOVEMENT

THIRD MOVEMENT

FOURTH MOVEMENT

HAYDN

Symphony No. 7, C major, B & H 97 1791-2

"LONDON NO. 1"

FIRST MOVEMENT

SECOND MOVEMENT

THIRD MOVEMENT (Menuetto)

FOURTH MOVEMENT

HAYDN

Symphony No. 8, Bb major, B & H 98 1792

"LONDON NO. 4"

FIRST MOVEMENT

SECOND MOVEMENT

[concluded on next page]

HAYDN

Symphony No. 8, Bb major, [concluded]

THIRD MOVEMENT Menuetto

FOURTH MOVEMENT

HAYDN

Symphony No. 9, C minor, B & H 95 *1791*

"LONDON NO. 5"

FIRST MOVEMENT

Allegro moderato

SECOND MOVEMENT

Andante cantabile

THIRD MOVEMENT   Menuetto

FOURTH MOVEMENT

Vivace

HAYDN

Symphony No. 10, D major, B & H 86 1786

FIRST MOVEMENT

SECOND MOVEMENT

THIRD MOVEMENT Menuetto

FOURTH MOVEMENT

HAYDN

Symphony No. 11, G major, B & H 100 *1794*

"MILITARY"

FIRST MOVEMENT

SECOND MOVEMENT

THIRD MOVEMENT Menuetto

FOURTH MOVEMENT

1

2

HAYDN

Symphony No. 12, Bb major, B & H 102 *1794–5*

"LONDON NO. 9"

FIRST MOVEMENT

SECOND MOVEMENT

THIRD MOVEMENT

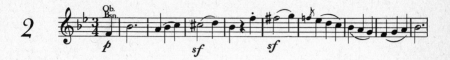

FOURTH MOVEMENT

HAYDN

Symphony No. 45, F♯ minor, B & H 18 *177*

"CANDLE" OR "FAREWELL"

FIRST MOVEMENT

SECOND MOVEMENT

THIRD MOVEMENT Menuetto

FOURTH MOVEMENT

FIFTH MOVEMENT

HILL
Symphony No. 2, C major, op. 35

FIRST MOVEMENT

SECOND MOVEMENT Scherzo

THIRD MOVEMENT

FOURTH MOVEMENT

2

HILL

Symphony No. 3, G major, OP. 41

FIRST MOVEMENT

Allegro giocoso ma con brio

1

2

SECOND MOVEMENT

Moderato non troppo lento

1

Pochissimo più mosso

2

THIRD MOVEMENT

1

2

HONEGGER

Symphony for Orchestra, *1929–30*

FIRST MOVEMENT

SECOND MOVEMENT

THIRD MOVEMENT

D'INDY

Symphony No. 2, Bb major, OP. 57

FIRST MOVEMENT

SECOND MOVEMENT

THIRD MOVEMENT

FOURTH MOVEMENT

MAHLER
Symphony No. 2, C minor *1894*
"RESURRECTION"

FIRST MOVEMENT

SECOND MOVEMENT

THIRD MOVEMENT

FOURTH MOVEMENT

FIFTH MOVEMENT

MAHLER

Symphony No. 3, D minor *1876*

FIRST MOVEMENT

SECOND MOVEMENT

3 L'istesso tempo as former *f* *staccato*

THIRD MOVEMENT

1 Comodo scherzando without haste *8va* Piccolo *tr* *f*

2 V. *pp*

3 L'istesso tempo (as former) Str. *ff* *ff*

4 Very comfortable (somewhat slower than former) Post Hn.

FOURTH MOVEMENT

1 Very slowly misterioso Vc. C.B. muted *ppp*

2 Alto solo Hn. *p* *molto espressivo*
Gib acht! Gib acht!
(*Take heed!* *Take heed!*)

[concluded on next page]

MAHLER

Symphony No. 3, D minor [concluded]

FIFTH MOVEMENT

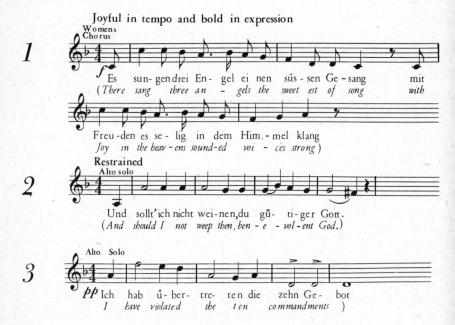

SIXTH MOVEMENT

MAHLER

Symphony No. 4, G major 1901

FIRST MOVEMENT

[concluded on next pages]

MAHLER

Symphony No. 4, G major [continued]

SECOND MOVEMENT

THIRD MOVEMENT

FOURTH MOVEMENT

MAHLER

Symphony No. 5, C♯ minor 1903

"GIANT"

FIRST MOVEMENT

SECOND MOVEMENT

THIRD MOVEMENT Scherzo

[concluded on next pages]

MAHLER

Symphony No. 5, C# minor [continued]

"GIANT"

3

4

5

FOURTH MOVEMENT

1

2

FIFTH MOVEMENT Rondo

Introductory

MASON

Symphony No. 3, Bb major, op. 35 *1935*

"LINCOLN"

FIRST MOVEMENT The young Lincoln

SECOND MOVEMENT "Massa Linkum"

THIRD MOVEMENT Old Abe's Yarns

FOURTH MOVEMENT

MENDELSSOHN

Symphony No. 3, A minor, op. 56 1842

"SCOTCH"

FIRST MOVEMENT

SECOND MOVEMENT

THIRD MOVEMENT

FOURTH MOVEMENT

MENDELSSOHN

Symphony No. 4, A major, op. 90 *1833*

"ITALIAN"

FIRST MOVEMENT

SECOND MOVEMENT

THIRD MOVEMENT

2

FOURTH MOVEMENT Saltarello

MENDELSSOHN

Symphony No. 5, D major, op. 107 *1829–30*

"REFORMATION"

FIRST MOVEMENT

SECOND MOVEMENT

THIRD MOVEMENT Part one

THIRD MOVEMENT Part two   A Mighty Fortress is Our God

THIRD MOVEMENT Part three

MOZART

Symphony No. 1, Eb major, K–16 1764

FIRST MOVEMENT

SECOND MOVEMENT

THIRD MOVEMENT

MOZART

Symphony No. 12, G major, K-110 1771

FIRST MOVEMENT

SECOND MOVEMENT

THIRD MOVEMENT

FOURTH MOVEMENT

MOZART

Symphony No. 35, D major, K–385 *1782*

"HAFFNER"

FIRST MOVEMENT

SECOND MOVEMENT

THIRD MOVEMENT

FOURTH MOVEMENT

MOZART

Symphony No. 36, C major, K–425 1783

"LINZ"

FIRST MOVEMENT

SECOND MOVEMENT

THIRD MOVEMENT

FOURTH MOVEMENT

MOZART

Symphony No. 37, G major, K–444 178

FIRST MOVEMENT

SECOND MOVEMENT

THIRD MOVEMENT

MOZART

Symphony No. 38, D major, K–504 *1786*

"PRAGUE—WITHOUT MINUET"

FIRST MOVEMENT

SECOND MOVEMENT

THIRD MOVEMENT

MOZART

Symphony No. 39, Eb major, K-543 1788

FIRST MOVEMENT

SECOND MOVEMENT

THIRD MOVEMENT Menuetto

[concluded on next page]

MOZART

Symphony No. 39, Eb major, [concluded]

FOURTH MOVEMENT

MOZART

Symphony No. 40, G minor, к–550 *1788*

FIRST MOVEMENT

SECOND MOVEMENT

THIRD MOVEMENT Menuetto

FOURTH MOVEMENT

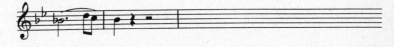

MOZART

Symphony No. 41, C major, K-551 *1788*

"JUPITER"

FIRST MOVEMENT

SECOND MOVEMENT

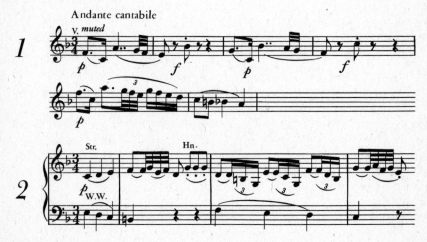

THIRD MOVEMENT

FOURTH MOVEMENT

PROKOFIEFF

Classical Symphony, D major, OP. 25 *1916–1*

FIRST MOVEMENT

SECOND MOVEMENT

PROKOFIEFF *Classical Symphony* D MAJOR [continued]

THIRD MOVEMENT

FOURTH MOVEMENT

203

RACHMANINOFF

Symphony No. 2, E minor, op. 27 1885–0

FIRST MOVEMENT

SECOND MOVEMENT

THIRD MOVEMENT

RACHMANINOFF *Symphony No. 2.* E MINOR [continued]

FOURTH MOVEMENT

SAINT-SAENS

Symphony No. 3, C minor, op. 78 1885–(

WITH ORGAN

FIRST MOVEMENT Part one

FIRST MOVEMENT Part two

SECOND MOVEMENT Scherzo   Part One

SECOND MOVEMENT   Part Two

SCHUBERT

Symphony No. 4, C minor *1816*

"TRAGIC"

FIRST MOVEMENT

SECOND MOVEMENT

THIRD MOVEMENT (Menuetto)

FOURTH MOVEMENT

SCHUBERT

Symphony No. 5, Bb major *1816*

FIRST MOVEMENT

SECOND MOVEMENT

THIRD MOVEMENT (Menuetto)

FOURTH MOVEMENT

SCHUBERT

Symphony No. 7, C major 1828

"GREAT"

FIRST MOVEMENT

SECOND MOVEMENT

THIRD MOVEMENT Scherzo

FOURTH MOVEMENT

SCHUBERT

Symphony No. 8, B minor 1822

"UNFINISHED"

FIRST MOVEMENT

SECOND MOVEMENT

SCHUMANN

Symphony No. 1, Bb major, OP. 38 1841

"SPRING"

FIRST MOVEMENT

SECOND MOVEMENT

THIRD MOVEMENT (Scherzo)

FOURTH MOVEMENT

SCHUMANN

Symphony No. 2, C major, op. 61   *1845–6*

FIRST MOVEMENT

SECOND MOVEMENT Scherzo

THIRD MOVEMENT

FOURTH MOVEMENT

SCHUMANN

Symphony No. 3, Eb major, OP. 97 *1850*

"RHENISH"

FIRST MOVEMENT

SECOND MOVEMENT Scherzo

THIRD MOVEMENT

FOURTH MOVEMENT

FIFTH MOVEMENT

SCHUMANN

Symphony No. 4, D minor, op. 120 *1841–5*

FIRST MOVEMENT

SECOND MOVEMENT (Romanze)

THIRD MOVEMENT (Scherzo)

FOURTH MOVEMENT

SHOSTAKOVICH

Symphony No. 1, Opus 10 *1927*

FIRST MOVEMENT

SECOND MOVEMENT

THIRD MOVEMENT

FOURTH MOVEMENT

SIBELIUS

Symphony No. 1, E minor, op. 39 *1899*

FIRST MOVEMENT

SECOND MOVEMENT

THIRD MOVEMENT Scherzo

FOURTH MOVEMENT

SIBELIUS

Symphony No. 2, D major, op. 43 *1902*

IN ONE MOVEMENT

SIBELIUS

Symphony No. 3, C major, op. 52 *1907*

FIRST MOVEMENT

SECOND MOVEMENT

THIRD MOVEMENT

SIBELIUS

Symphony No. 4, A minor, op. 63 *1912*

FIRST MOVEMENT

SECOND MOVEMENT

THIRD MOVEMENT

FOURTH MOVEMENT

SIBELIUS

Symphony No. 5, Eb major, op. 82 *1915*

FIRST MOVEMENT

SECOND MOVEMENT

THIRD MOVEMENT

SIBELIUS

Symphony No. 6, D minor, op. 104 *1923*

FIRST MOVEMENT

SECOND MOVEMENT

THIRD MOVEMENT

FOURTH MOVEMENT

SIBELIUS

Symphony No. 7, C major OP. 105 *1925*

FIRST MOVEMENT

SECOND MOVEMENT

THIRD MOVEMENT

FOURTH MOVEMENT

SOWERBY

Symphony No. 2

FIRST MOVEMENT

SECOND MOVEMENT

THIRD MOVEMENT (Fugue)

STRAUSS, RICHARD

Alpine Symphony, Bb minor, op. 64 *1915*

FIRST MOVEMENT

[concluded on next pages]

STRAUSS, RICHARD

Alpine Symphony, Bb minor, [continued]

SECOND MOVEMENT

THIRD MOVEMENT

STRAUSS, RICHARD

Aus Italien, G major, op. 16 *1886*

FIRST MOVEMENT (On the Campagna)

SECOND MOVEMENT (Amid Romes Ruines)

THIRD MOVEMENT On the Shores of Sorrento

FOURTH MOVEMENT Neapolitan Popular Life

STRINGHAM

Symphony No. 1, B♭ minor, *1929*

FIRST MOVEMENT

SECOND MOVEMENT

THIRD MOVEMENT

TCHAIKOVSKY
Symphony No. 3, D major, OP. 29 *1875*
"POLISH"

FIRST MOVEMENT

SECOND MOVEMENT

THIRD MOVEMENT

FOURTH MOVEMENT Scherzo

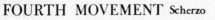

FIFTH MOVEMENT

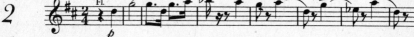

TCHAIKOVSKY

Symphony No. 4, F minor, op. 36 *1877*

FIRST MOVEMENT

SECOND MOVEMENT

THIRD MOVEMENT   Scherzo

FOURTH MOVEMENT

TCHAIKOVSKY

Symphony No. 5, E minor, op. 64 *1888*

FIRST MOVEMENT

SECOND MOVEMENT

THIRD MOVEMENT

FOURTH MOVEMENT

TCHAIKOVSKY

Symphony No. 6, B minor, op. 74 *1893*

"PATHÉTIQUE"

FIRST MOVEMENT

SECOND MOVEMENT

THIRD MOVEMENT

FOURTH MOVEMENT

VAUGHAN WILLIAMS

London Symphony, *1912–13*

FIRST MOVEMENT

SECOND MOVEMENT

THIRD MOVEMENT

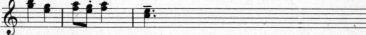

FOURTH MOVEMENT

VAUGHAN WILLIAMS

Pastoral, *1922*

FIRST MOVEMENT

SECOND MOVEMENT

THIRD MOVEMENT

FOURTH MOVEMENT

VAUGHAN WILLIAMS

Symphony, F minor *1931–4*

FIRST MOVEMENT

SECOND MOVEMENT

THIRD MOVEMENT Scherzo

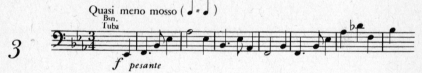

FOURTH MOVEMENT

A List of Recordings

I N CHOOSING the accompanying list of recorded examples of
the symphonies, an endeavor has been made to include
only first-rate versions that are easily obtainable. Also, I have
avoided including versions by certain famous conductors
whose name appeal is strong, but whose readings are highly
personalized or poorly recorded. Many fine recordings have
had to be omitted because they are not generally available
due to the world conditions that have curtailed their impor-
tation at this time. In striving to pick only the best, the first
consideration has been interpretation and, second, recording.

If a symphony has been recorded only once, that recording,
regardless of quality, is listed. The omission of a symphony
from the following list means, of course, that it has not been
recorded.

The following symbols have been chosen to designate the
quality of recording: A—good; B—fair; C—poor.

GEORGE CLARK LESLIE

New York, April 16, 1941

Code symbols used in indentifying the recordings listed:

VM   Victor Masterpiece Set

CM   Columbia Masterwork Set

V   Victor 12″ double-faced disc

D   American Decca 12″ double-faced disc

D-CA   Imported British Decca-Polydor recording

†   Available in automatic sequence

List of Recommended Recordings

THE PUBLISHER *of this volume has asked George
Clark Leslie, editor of* The Gramophone Shop

Encyclopedia, *to prepare a list of the best and most available recordings of the symphonies whose themes appear in this volume. They follow below.*

BEETHOVEN

Symphony No. 1, in C Major, Opus 21
Vienna Philharmonic Orchestra—F. Weingartner CM-321†
Weingartner's readings of Beethoven are accepted as standard. A

Symphony No. 2, in D Major, Opus 36
London Philharmonic—Sir Thomas Beecham   CM-302†
An outstanding interpretation by England's greatest conductor. A

Symphony No. 3, in E Flat Major, Opus 55—"Eroica"
New York Philharmonic—Symphony Orchestra—Bruno Walter CM-449†
A sincere and eloquent performance, enhanced by superior recording. A

Symphony No. 4, in B Flat Minor, Opus 60
BBC Symphony Orchestra—Arturo Toscanini   VM-676†
Toscanini leads the BBC Symphony in a first-rate reading. A

Symphony No. 5, in C Minor, Opus 67
London Philharmonic Orchestra—F. Weingartner CM-254†
The standard interpretation of this popular work, which has been effectively recorded. A
Berlin Philharmonic Orchestra—W. Furtwängler VM-426†
An individual but stimulating approach to this work that has been highly acclaimed by musicians. A

Symphony No. 6, in F Major, Opus 68—"Pastoral"
BBC Symphony Orchestra—Arturo Toscanini   VM-417†
One of Toscanini's more celebrated readings. A

Symphony No. 7, in A Major, Opus 92
New York Philharmonic—Symphony Orchestra—Toscanini VM-317†

A spirited reading which many prefer to the standard version that follows.   A

Vienna Philharmonic Orchestra—F. Weingartner CM-260† B

Symphony No. 8, in F Major, Opus 93

Vienna Philharmonic Orchestra—F. Weingartner CM-292†

One of the loveliest of all of Weingartner's performances.   A

Symphony No. 9, in D Minor, Opus 125—"Choral"

Vienna Philharmonic Orchestra with Soloists and Chorus—
F. Weingartner CM-227†

Although not the latest recording, this version is the only one that fully captures the spirit of this work.   B

BERLIOZ
Symphony fantastique, in C Major, Opus 14

Paris Conservatory Orchestra—Bruno Walter   VM-662†

A good recording, but the reading is not as penetrating as we would wish.   A

BORODIN
Symphony No. 2, in B Minor, Opus 5

London Symphony Orchestra—Albert Coates   VM-113†

A masterful reading by the great Anglo-Russian conductor.   B

BRAHMS
Symphony No. 1, in C Minor, Opus 68

London Symphony Orchestra—F. Weingartner   CM-383†

Another composer's works that have been a foundation for Weingartner's remarkable reputation.   A

Symphony No. 2, in D Major, Opus 73

London Philharmonic Orchestra—Sir Thomas Beecham CM-265†

Beecham gives a spirited account of Brahms' second.   A

Symphony No. 3, in F Major, Opus 90

Chicago Symphony Orchestra—Frederick Stock   CM-443†

Stock's interpretations of Brahms has been highly acclaimed on this side of the Atlantic.   A

Symphony No. 4, in E Minor, Opus 98

London Symphony Orchestra—F. Weingartner   CM-335 †
*A first-rate recording and performance by the renowned Dalmatian
conductor.*   A

BRUCKNER
Symphony No. 4, in E Flat Major, Opus 62— "Romantic"

Saxon State Orchestra—Karl Böhm   VM-331 †
*A work that must be heard to be fully appreciated. Played by
a European conductor who habitually included Bruckner's
works on his programs, we have a fine interpretation.*   A

Symphony No. 7, in E Major, Opus 65

Minneapolis Symphony Orchestra—Eugene Ormandy
VM-276 †
*This is the only American recording of this work, and it is played
with great appreciation.*   B

Symphony No. 9, in D Minor, Opus 67

Munich Philharmonic Orchestra—S. von Hausegger VM-627 †
*This recording uses the original edition and not the usual version
prepared by Bruckner's disciple, Ferdinand Loewe.*   A

CHAUSSON
Symphony in B Flat Major, Opus 20

Paris Conservatory Orchestra—Pietro Coppola   VM-261 †
*Coppola, the noted French conductor, gives a thoroughly enjoyable
reading of this score.*   B

DVOŘÁK
Symphony No. 4, in G Major, Opus 88

Czech Philharmonic—V. Talich   VM-304 †
A fine score that deserves to be better known.   A

Symphony No. 5, in E Minor, Opus 95—"From the New World"

Czech Philharmonic—G. Szell   VM-469 †
*The one and only interpretation devoid of excess sentiment.
Played and recorded by Czech artists which gives us Dvořák's
view of the "New World" as he wished it to be played.*   A

FRANCK

Symphony in D Minor

Philadelphia Orchestra—L. Stokowski VM-300†

Stokowski's mannered reading is far from the intention of composer, but it is the best of the few versions easily obtained. B

Lamoreux Orchestra—A. Wolff D-CA8128/31

Wolff's reading is essentially "Gallic" and therefore very close to the spirit of the work. Not a new recording but one which is preferable to the Stokowski version listed above. B

GOLDMARK

Symphony in E Flat Major, Opus 26—"Rustic Wedding"

CB Symphony—H. Barlow CM-385†

A refreshing and well-played version of this well-known work. A

HANSON

Symphony No. 2, in C Major, Opus 30—"Romantic"

Eastman-Rochester Symphony Orchestra—H. Hanson
VM-648†

An authoritative reading revealed by the composer. A

HARRIS

Symphony No. 3

Boston Symphony—S. Koussevitzky VM-651

Victor's recording engineers have captured with utmost fidelity Koussevitzky's reading of one of Harris' most discussed works. A

HAYDN

Symphony No. 103, in E Flat Major—"Drum Roll"

St. Louis Symphony—V. Golschmann CM-221

Not a good recording, but the only one available. C

Symphony No. 104, in D Major—"London"

London Philharmonic—Beecham CM-409†

The eminent Sir Thomas fully reveals this fine score. A

Symphony No. 99, in E Flat Major—"Imperial"

London Philharmonic—Beecham CM-264†

Sir Thomas in another of his unsurpassable readings of Haydn. A

Symphony No. 101, in D Major—"Clock"

New York Philharmonic-Symphony Society—A. Toscanini
VM-57†

The standard version for these many years and not likely to be bettered. B

Symphony No. 93, in D Major

London Philharmonic—Beecham CM-336†

The same story: Haydn and Beecham ensure a superb set of disks. A

Symphony No. 94, in G Major—"Surprise"

Boston Symphony—S. Koussevitzky VM-55†

A superlative reading which holds its own, in spite of oldish recording. B

CB Symphony—H. Barlow CM-363†

Mr. Barlow gives a vivacious account of this work and is aided by very fine recording. For those who must have the newest. B

Symphony No. 97, in C Major

London Symphony—H. Weisbach VM-140†

The only available recording. C

Symphony No. 98, in B Flat Major

CB Symphony—H. Barlow CM-370†

An excellent set by Mr. Barlow and the CB Symphony, which has been given first-rate recording. A

Symphony No. 95, in C Minor

London Symphony—H. Harty D-25598/99

A short work to which the late Sir Hamilton Harty gave an eloquent interpretation. B

Symphony No. 86, in D Major

London Symphony Orchestra—B. Walter VM-578†

Walter's readings of Haydn are very interesting, and this one is especially fine. B

Symphony No. 100, in G Major—"Military"

Vienna Philharmonic—B. Walter VM-472†

Recorded with Walter's own orchestra in Vienna, this set is recommended, for it is the only good recording available, though not too well played. B

Symphony No. 102, in B Flat Major
Boston Symphony—S. Koussevitzky VM-529†
One of Koussevitzky's expert performances of Haydn. A

Symphony No. 45, in F Sharp Minor—"Farewell"
London Symphony—H. Wood CM-205
A pleasant recording of a delightful work. C

MAHLER
Symphony No. 2, in C Minor—"Resurrection"
Minneapolis Symphony with Soloists and Chorus—E. Ormandy VM-256†
A pioneering recording of this work which has met with great success. The contralto solo in the 4th movement is one of the most moving of Mahler's inspirations. B

Symphony No. 5, in C Sharp Minor—"Giant"
Second Movement (only)—Adagietto
Vienna Philharmonic—B. Walter V-12319
Scored for strings and harp, this movement has been given beautiful recording. B

MENDELSSOHN
Symphony No. 3, in A Minor, Opus 56—"Scotch"
Rochester Philharmonic—J. Iturbi VM-699†
Iturbi's debut as a conductor, and he gives a very stimulating account of this well-known work. A

Symphony No. 4, in A Major, Opus 90—"Italian"
Boston Symphony—S. Koussevitzky VM-294†
Koussevitzky gives a very fine reading of the "Italian." B

Symphony No. 5, in D Major, Opus 107—"The Reformation"
CB Symphony—H. Barlow CM-391†
Mr. Barlow and the CB Symphony play this work in a most pleasing manner. A

MOZART
Symphony No. 35, in D Major, K. 385—"Haffner"
London Philharmonic—Beecham CM-399†
Sir Thomas' Mozart readings are things of rare beauty which can be equaled by few, but not surpassed by any. A

New York Philharmonic-Symphony Society—A. Toscanini
VM-65†
*An early electrical recording by Toscanini which shows him at
the height of his interpretative ability. A reading very similar
to Beecham's, listed above.*   B

Symphony No. 36, in C Major, K. 425—"Linz"

London Philharmonic—Beecham   CM-387†
Another of Sir Thomas's superb readings and recordings.   A

Symphony No. 38, in D Major, K. 457—"Prague"

Chicago Symphony Orchestra—F. Stock   CM-410†
*The best reading and recording of this work until the Beecham
version which is available in England is released to the American record buyer. Definitely superior to the existing Walter
version.*   B

Symphony No. 39, in E Flat Major, K. 543

BBC Symphony—B. Walter   VM-258
*Walter leads the BBC Symphony in a very satisfactory version of
this work.*   A

Symphony No. 40, in G Minor, K. 550

London Philharmonic—Beecham   CM-316
*Superior in every respect. Beecham has been given much the best
recording of any existing version. Toscanini (VM-631), with
NBC Orchestra, is definitely out—except to his most ardent
admirers—because of Studio 8H recording.*   A

Symphony No. 41, in C Major, K. 551—"Jupiter"

London Philharmonic—Beecham   CM-194
*Although the oldest recording, this version by Sir Thomas is
superior to the reading by the Vienna Philharmonic-Walter
(VM-584).*   A

PROKOFIEFF
Symphony in D Major, Opus 25—"Classical"

Boston Symphony Orchestra—S. Koussevitzky   V-7196/7
*Koussevitzky catches the humor and wit of this delightful work
and although his version is not too recent, it is superior to the
Minneapolis-Mitropoulos (CM-X166) reading which does not
seem to convey any of the above-mentioned characteristics.*   A

RACHMANINOFF
Symphony No. 2, in E Minor, Opus 27
Minneapolis Symphony—E. Ormandy   VM-239
Ormandy gives a telling account of this little-heard work.   A

SAINT-SAËNS
Symphony No. 3, in C Minor, Opus 78
Symphony Orchestra with Organ and two Pianos—P. Coppola   VM-100
This, the only available recording, is somewhat dated.   B

SCHUBERT
Symphony No. 4, in C Minor—"Tragic"
New York Philharmonic-Symphony Society—Barbirolli VM-562†
A recording by Barbirolli that can be fully recommended.   B

Symphony No. 5, in B Flat Major
London Philharmonic—Beecham   CM-366†
Sir Thomas gives a particularly inspired account of this charming work, which has been given perfect recording.   A

Symphony No. 9 (Old No. 7), in C Major—"Great"
Chicago Symphony—F. Stock   CM-403†
It is a close choice between this extremely fine reading by Stock and the Chicago Symphony and the London Symphony—B. Walter (VM-602) version. However, we feel that the Chicago Orchestra has been better recorded.   A

Symphony No. 8, in B Minor—"Unfinished"
London Philharmonic—Beecham   CM-330†
Beecham, who has given the problems of recording careful study, triumphs again with a set of finely recorded disks of his noteworthy reading.   A

SCHUMANN
Symphony No. 1, in B Flat Major, Opus 38—"Spring"
Boston Symphony—S. Koussevitzky   VM-655†
One of the finest recordings to come from Symphony Hall.   A

Symphony No. 2, in C Major, Opus 61
Philadelphia Orchestra—E. Ormandy   VM-448†
Ormandy and his men give an inspired account which has been faithfully recorded.   B

Symphony No. 3, in E Flat Major, Opus 97—"Rhenish"

Paris Conservatory Orchestra—P. Coppola VM-237†
An adequate performance of this work. C

SHOSTAKOVICH
Symphony No. 1, Opus 10

Philadelphia Orchestra—L. Stokowski VM-192†
*Stokowski made the first American recording of Shostakovich's
works. A labor of love, for the passing of time has left its
trace.* B

SIBELIUS
Symphony No. 1, in E Minor, Opus 39

Symphony Orchestra—R. Kajanus CM-151
*In spite of oldish recording, this version is preferable to the newer
one by Ormandy-Minneapolis (VM-290). Kajanus, a close
friend of Sibelius, is said to come closest to the composer's
intentions.* B

Symphony No. 2, in D Major, Opus 43

Symphony Orchestra—R. Kajanus CM-149—B
Boston Symphony—S. Koussevitzky VM-272†—B
*Both conductors give inspired accounts of the score, but those who
prefer more recent recording should choose the Koussevitzky
version.*

Symphony No. 3, in C Major, Opus 52

London Symphony—R. Kajanus VM-394†
The standard gramophonic version, by the late Robert Kajanus.
B

Symphony No. 4, in A Minor, Opus 63

London Philharmonic—Beecham VM-446†
*Sir Thomas, besides being a friend to the older composers, turns
in a deft performance of Sibelius too.* A

Symphony No. 5, in E Flat Major, Opus 82

Boston Symphony—S. Koussevitzky VM-474†
*Koussevitzky's reading of the 5th has superceded the former
version by Kajanus.* A

Symphony No. 6, in D Minor, Opus 104

Finnish National Orchestra—G. Schneevoight VM-344†
The standard version. B

Symphony No. 7, in C Major, Opus 105

BBC Symphony—Koussevitzky VM-394†

Koussevitzky's fine interpretation is included in the same album with Symphony No. 3, listed above. A

TCHAIKOVSKY

Symphony No. 3, in D Major, Opus 29—"Polish"

National Symphony Orchestra—H. Kindler VM-747†

Kindler and his orchestra give a first-rate performance of this work which has been accorded excellent treatment by the engineers. A *An older version by London Symphony-Coates (VM-166) is still available, but the recording is dated.*

Symphony No. 4, in F Minor, Opus 36

Boston Symphony—S. Koussevitzky VM-327†

Koussevitzky and his men give this popular work an inspired reading. A

Symphony No. 5, in E Minor, Opus 64

The Cleveland Orchestra—A. Rodzinski CM-406†

Newcomers to the list, but Dr. Rodzinski is one of the finest of the younger conductors. Here he gives us a top-notch account of the score, omitting all the "sentimental excesses" that are frequently read into these pages. Recording is excellent. A

Symphony No. 6, in B Minor, Opus 74—"Pathétique"

Berlin Philharmonic—W. Furtwängler VM-553

Once again a fresh approach can reveal more of the score than all of the studied and personal readings. Here we have the best of the all-too-numerous versions. A

VAUGHAN WILLIAMS

London Symphony

Queen's Hall Orchestra—H. Wood (Five 12″ disks)
D-25618/22

The revised version of this work has been effectively recorded by Sir Henry. B

Symphony in F Minor

BBC Symphony—Vaughan Williams VM-440

An authentic reading by the composer. B

Dictionary of Musical Terms

Adagio = slowly
Affrettuoso = hurry
Agitato = agitated
Alla breve = with ♩ beat
Alla marcia = like a march
Allegretto = slightly slower than allegro
Allegro = cheerfully
Andante = going
Andantino = going a little
Animato = animated
Animez = animated
Appass. = *Appassionato* = passionately
Assai = rather
A tempo = up to tempo

Ben = well
Brillante = brilliantly
Brio = brilliance

Calmo = calmly
Cant. = *Cantabile* = in singing style
Cantando = in singing style
Circa = about
Comodo = comfortably
Con = with
Con alcuna licenza = with some freedom
Cresc. = *Crescendo* = increasingly louder

Deciso = with decision
Delicato = delicately

Devozione = with devotion
Dignito = with dignity
Dim. = increasingly softer
Dol. = *Dolce* = sweetly
Dolcezza = sweetly
Dolcissimo = as sweetly as possible
Dolente = sadly
Dolorosamente = very sadly
Dolorosa = sadly
Doppio piu lento = doubly more slowly

E = and
Ed = and
Elegiaco = elegiacal
Energia = energy
Energico = energetically
Espansione = expansively
Espr. = *Espressivo* = expressively

f = *Forte* = loud
Feroce = ferociously
ff = *Fortissimo* = as loudly as possible
ffz = suddenly very loud
Flebile = plaintive, mournful
fp = loud, then suddenly soft
Fuoco = fire
fz = suddenly loud

Giocoso = jokingly
Grave = serious, slow
Grazia = grace
Grazioso = gracefully

275

In modo di canzone = in the manner of a song

Lamentoso = lamentingly
La melodia = the melody
Largamente = broadly
Larghetto = rather broadly
Largo = broadly
Legato = smoothly
Leggieramente = lightly
Leggiero = lightly
Legière = (French) lightly
Lenezza = gentleness
Lent = slowly
L'istesso tempo = at the same tempo
Lugubre = lugubriously

Ma = but
Maestoso = majestically
Marc. = *Marcato* = marked
Marcatissimo = marked as much as possible
Marcia = march
Marcia funebre = funeral march
Meno = less
Meno mosso = less motion
Mezza voce = half voice
mf = *mezzo forte* = moderately loud
Misterioso = mysteriously
Moderato = moderately
Molto = very
Moto = motion
mp = *mezzo piano* = moderately soft

Nobilmente = nobly
Non tanto = not so much
Non troppo = not too much

Ova = at the octave
Ostinato = persistent, stubborn

p = *piano* = softly
Passionato = passionately
Pesante = heavy
Piangendo = weeping, crying
Pianissimo = as softly as possible
Più = more
Più mosso = more motion
Pizz. = pizzicato
Pizzicato = plucked
Pochettino = very little
Pochissimo = as little as possible
Poco = a little
Poco a poco = little by little
pp = *pianissimo* = as softly as possible
Prestissimo = as fast as possible
Presto = fast

Quasi = almost like

Risoluto = resolutely
Rit. = ritard
Ritardando = slowing down
Ritmico = rhythmically
Rubato = robbing — rhythmic expression

Scherzando = playfully
Semplice = simply
Sempre = always
Senza misura = without measures
sf = *sforzando* = sudden accent
Slentando = to slacken
Sonoramente = sonorously
Sonore = sonorously
Sost. = *sostenuto* = sustained
Sostenuto = sustained

276

Sotto voce = softly
Spiccato = detached
Spirito = with spirit
Spiritoso = with spirit
Stacc. = *staccato* = cut off
Stretto = faster
Suave = suavely
Sub. = *subito* = suddenly
Supplice = suppliantly

Tempo = speed of the beat
Tempo del comincio = tempo of the beginning
Tempo di menuetto = tempo of a minuet

Tempo di polacca = tempo of a polonaise
Tempo di valse = tempo of a waltz
Teneramente = tenderly
Tenuto = held, sustained
Tr = trill
Tranquillo = quietly
Trem = tremolo
Tutta forza = all force

Un poco = a little

Vivace = vivaciously
Vivacissimo = as fast as possible
Vivo = lively

Bibliography

ABELL, ARTHUR M. "Analysis of the Alpine Symphony," *Musical Courier*, v. 71, No. 23, pp. 5–7. New York: Dec. 9, 1915.

ABRAHAM, GERALD. *Borodin, the Composer and his Music*. London: W. Reeves, 1927.

BLOM, ERIC. (Tchaikovsky's) "Symphony No. 4 in F minor, Op. 36," *Musical Pilgrim*, v. 25, pp. 23–42. London: Oxford University Press, 1927.

BOROWSKI, FELIX. *See* UPTON, GEORGE P., and BOROWSKI, FELIX

BRIAN, HAVERGAL. "Anton Bruckner's 'Romantic' Symphony No. 4," *Musical Opinion*, v. 52, No. 614, pp. 147–49. London: Nov. 1928.

BROWNE, PHILLIP A. "Brahms, the Symphonies," *Musical Pilgrim*, v. 32. London: Oxford University Press, 1935.

COLLES, HENRY COPE. "Symphony and the Drama, 1850–1900," Chaps. 5–7, *Oxford History of Music*, v. 7. London: Oxford University Press, 1933.

DANNREUTHER, EDWARD. "The Romantic Period," Chaps. 6–7, *Oxford History of Music*, v. 6. London: Oxford University Press, 1931.

DICKENSON, ALAN E. F. "A Study of Mozart's Last Three Symphonies, *Musical Pilgrim*, v. 12. London: Oxford University Press, 1927.

———. "An Introduction to the Music of R. Vaughan Williams," *Musical Pilgrim*, v. 18. London: Oxford University Press, 1928.

DONALD, PAUL. "Richard Strauss' Symphonic Tone Poem, No. I; Symphonic Fantasy—*Aus Italien*, Op. 16," *Metronome*, v. 31, No. 1, pp. 42–43. New York: Jan., 1915.

———. "Great Orchestral Works by Modern Composers: No. 17, Symphony, *Rustic Wedding*, Op. 26, by Karl Goldmark," *Metronome*, v. 33, No. 8, pp. 42–43. New York: Aug., 1917.

———. "Great Orchestral Works by Modern Composers: No. 22, Symphony No. 6 in B minor, 'Pathétique,' Op. 74, by Peter Tschaikowsky," *Metronome*, v. 34, No. 7, p. 45; No. 8, pp. 43, 60–61. New York: July–Aug., 1918.

———. "Great Orchestral Works by Modern Composers: No. 27, Symphony in D minor for Orchestra, by César Franck," *Metronome*, v. 35, No. 5, pp. 44–45; No. 7, pp. 25, 53–55. New York: May, July, 1919.

DOWNES, OLIN. "Mason Symphony on Lincoln Given," *The New York Times*. New York: Nov. 18, 1937.

————. *Symphonic Masterpieces*. New York: The Dial Press, 1935.

ELLIOT, JOHN HAROLD. *Berlioz*. London: J. M. Dent & Sons, Ltd., 1938.

EMERICK, ALBERT G. *Celebrated Musical Works*. Philadelphia: John Pennington & Son, 1871.

EVANS, EDWIN. *Beethoven's Nine Symphonies*. 2 v. London: W. Reeves, 1923.

————. *Handbook to the Chamber and Orchestral Music of Johannes Brahms*. 2 v. London: W. Reeves, Ltd., 1933.

————. *Tchaikovsky*, in "Master Musicians" series. London: J. M. Dent & Sons, Ltd., 1st. ed. 1906; revised ed. 1935.

FINCK, HENRY T. *Richard Strauss, the Man and his Works*. Boston: Little, Brown & Co., 1917.

FOX, DOUGLAS GERARD. "Joseph Haydn (an introduction)," *Musical Pilgrim*, v. 20, pp. 9–27. London: Oxford University Press, 1929.

FOX, STRANGWAYS A. H. "Ralph Vaughan Williams," *Music and Letters*, v. 1, pp. 81–82. London: April, 1920.

GODDARD, SCOTT. "Sivelius' Second Symphony," *Music and Letters*, v. 12, pp. 156–163. London: April, 1931.

GOEPP, PHILIP H. *Symphonies and Their Meanings*, ser. 1–3. Philadelphia: J. B. Lippincott, 1898–1913.

GOETSCHIUS, PERCY. *Analytic Symphony Series*. Boston: Oliver Ditson Co., 1927–37.

————. *Masters of the Symphony*. Boston: Oliver Ditson Co., 1929.

GOODRICH, ALFRED JOHN. *Complete Musical Analysis*. Cincinnati: The John Church Co., 1889.

GRAMOPHONE SHOP, INC. *The Gramophone Shop Encyclopedia of Recorded Music*. New York: The Gramophone Shop, Inc., 1936.

————. "Record Supplement." New York: The Gramophone Shop, Inc., Nov., 1937, to date.

GRAY, CECIL. *Sibelius*. London: Oxford University Press, 1931.

————. "The Symphonies," *Musical Pilgrim*, v. 35. London: Oxford University Press, 1935.

GROVE, SIR GEORGE. *Beethoven and His Nine Symphonies*. London: Novello & Co., Ltd., 1896.

————. "Mendelssohn's 'Italian' Symphony," *Musical Times*, v. 47, pp. 244–47. London: April 1, 1906.

————. "Mendelssohn's 'Scotch' Symphony in A minor, Op. 56," *Musical Times*, v. 45, pp. 644–46; 717–19. London: Oct. 1, 1904.

————. "Mozart's Symphony in C (the 'Jupiter')," *Musical Times*, v. 47, pp. 27–31. London: Jan. 1, 1906.

————. "Mozart's Symphony in G minor," *Musical Times*, v. 48, pp. 25–28. London: Jan. 1, 1907.

————. "Schubert's 'Great' Symphony in C," *Musical Times*, v. 45, pp. 523–28. London: Aug. 1, 1904.

————. "Schubert's 'Unfinished' Symphony in B minor," *Musical Times*, v. 48, pp. 790–92. London: Dec. 1, 1907.

————. "Schumann's Symphony in B flat," *Musical Times*, v. 49, pp. 384–87. London: June 1, 1908.

————. "Schumann's Symphony in E flat (the 'Rhenish.'), Op. 97," *Musical Times*, v. 50, pp. 789–92. London: Dec. 1, 1909.

————. "Sir Edward Elgar's Symphony," *Musical Times*, v. 49, pp. 778–80. London: Dec. 1, 1908.

————. "The First Symphony of Brahms in C minor, Op. 68," *Times*, v. 46, pp. 318–20. London: June 1, 1905.

HAGGIN, BERNARD H. *A Book of the Symphony*. London: Oxford University Press, 1937.

HALE, PHILIP. *Boston Symphony Program Notes*. Garden City, N. Y.: Doubleday, Doran Co., Inc., 1935.

HARVEY, ARTHUR. *Saint-Saëns*. London: John Lane, Ltd., 1921.

HOFFMEISTER, KAREL. *Antonín Dvořák*. London: John Lane, Ltd., 1928.

HOWELLS, HERBERT. "Vaughan Williams' 'Pastoral' Symphony," *Music and Letters*, v. 3, pp. 122–32. London: April, 1922.

HOWES, FRANK. "Symphony in F minor," *Musical Pilgrim*, v. 37, pp. 46–62. London: Oxford University Press, 1937.

HULL, ROBERT H. *A Handbook on Arnold Bax's Symphonies*. London: Murdock, Murdock & Co., 1932.

————. "Bax's Third Symphony," *Musical Times*, v. 71, pp. 217–20. London: Mar. 1, 1930.

KAUFMAN, SHIMA. *Everybody's Music*. New York: Thomas Y. Crowell Co., 1938.

LEE, ERNEST M. "Tchaikovski," *Music of the Masters*, pp. 1–31. New York: Bretano's, 1904.

LYLE, WATSON. *Camille Saint-Saëns*. London: Paul, Trench, Trübner & Co., Ltd., 1923.

MAINE, BASIL S. *Elgar, His Life and Works*, 2 v. London: G. Bell & Sons, Ltd., 1933.

MARTENS, FREDERIC H. *Little Biographies*. New York: Breitkopf Publications, Inc., 1921–25.

MASON, DANIEL GREGORY. *Contemporary Composers*. New York: The Macmillan Co., 1918.

————. *The Romantic Composers*. New York: The Macmillan Co., 1906.

————. "The Appreciation of Music," vol. 3, *Short Studies of Great Masterpieces*. New York: The H. W. Gray Co., 1918.

————. "Symphony in D minor, by César Franck," *New Musical Review*, v. 16, No. 184, pp. 502–05. New York: Mar., 1917.

————. "Symphony No. 3 in C minor, by Camille Saint-Saëns," *New Musical Review*, v. 16, No. 188, pp. 646–50. New York: July, 1917.

————. "Symphony No. 3 in F major, by Johannes Brahms," *New Music Review*, v. 16, No. 181, pp. 390–94. New York: Dec., 1916.

————. "Symphony No. 5, 'From the New World,' by Antonín Dvořák," *New Music Review*, v. 16, No. 189, pp. 682–86. New York: Aug., 1917.

————. "Symphony No. 6, '*Pathétique*,' by Peter Tschaikowsky," *New Music Review*, v. 16, No. 186, pp. 574–78. New York: May, 1917.

MATHEWS, W. S. B. *The Great in Music*. Chicago: Music Magazine Pub. Co., 1900.

MEISSNER, WILLIAM O. *A Guide to Symphonic Music*. New York: Silver, Burdett Co., 1936.

MURPHY, HOWARD A. *The Symphonies of L. van Beethoven*. New York: Edwin F. Kalmus, 1939.

NEWMAN, ERNEST. "Elgar's Second Symphony," *Musical Times*, v. 52, pp. 295–300. London: May, 1911

NEWMARCH, ROSA H. *The Concert Goer's Library of Descriptive Notes*, v. 1, 4–5. London: Oxford University Press, 1928–33.

————. *Tchaikovsky's Life and Analyses of his Works*. London: W. Reeves, 1908.

O'CONNELL, CHARLES. *The Victor Book of the Symphony*. New York: Simon & Schuster, 1934; revised edition, 1941.

OSBORNE, ALONZO S. *Centuries of Progress in Music*. Ann Arbor, Mich: Edwards Bros., Inc., 1937.

PORTE, JOHN F. *Sir Edward Elgar*. New York: E. P. Dutton & Co., 1921.

————. *Some Famous Symphonies*. London: W. Reeves, 1927.

PROUT, EBENEZER. "Schumann's Symphony in B flat," *Monthly Musical Record*, v. 2, pp. 30–33. London: Mar. 1872.

————. "Schumann's Symphony in C major," *Monthly Musical Record*, v. 2, pp. 62–66. London: May, 1872.

————. "Schumann's Symphony in E flat," *Monthly Musical Record*, v. 2, pp. 77–81. London: June, 1872.

————. "Schumann's Symphony in D minor," *Monthly Musical Record*, v. 2, pp. 46–49. London: April, 1872.

R.C.A. MANUFACTURING CO., INC. *Catalogue of Victor Records*. Camden, N. J.: R.C.A. Manufacturing Co., Inc., 1938.

SCHIRMER, G., INC. *The Eulenberg Edition of Miniature Scores*. New York: 1939.

SHERA, FRANK H. "Elgar, Instrumental Works," *Musical Pilgrim*, v. 29, London: Oxford University Press, 1931.

SMITH, ALEXANDER BRENT. "Schubert," *Musical Pilgrim*, v. 15, London: Oxford University Press, 1926.

SPAETH, SIGMUND G. *Great Symphonies*. Garden City, N. Y.: Garden City Pub. Co., 1936.

STEFAN, PAUL. *Gustav Mahler*, New York: G. Schirmer, Inc., 1913.

THOMPSON, OSCAR. *The International Cyclopedia of Music and Musicians*. New York: Dodd, Mead & Co., 1939.

TOVEY, DONALD F. *Essays in Musical Analysis*. v. 1–2. London: Oxford University Press, 1935–37.

TRETBAR, CHARLES F. *Analytical Reviews of Classical and Modern Compositions*. New York: Charles F. Tretbar, 1877–78.

UPTON, GEORGE P., AND BOROWSKI, FELIX. *The Standard Concert Guide*. Chicago: A. C. McClurg & Co., 1930.

UPTON, GEORGE P. *The Standard Symphonies*. Chicago: A. C. McClurg & Co., 1891.

VAUGHAN WILLIAMS, RALPH. "London Symphony by Vaughan Williams," *British Musician*, v. 2, No. 4, pp. 149–56. West Bromwich, Eng: Dec., 1926.

WOTTEN, TOM S. "Berlioz," *Musical Pilgrim*, v. 21. London: Oxford University Press, 1929.

Index According to Keys

KEYS	COMPOSER	SYMPHONY NO.	PAGE
D minor	Franck		118
"	Hadley	4	124
"	Mahler	3	164
"	Schumann	4	222
"	Sibelius	6	236
E♭ major	Beethoven	3	62
"	Bruckner	4	100
"	Elgar	2	116
"	Goldmark	*Rustic Wedding*	122
"	Haydn	1	132
"	Haydn	3	136
"	Mozart	1	183
"	Mozart	39	194
"	Schumann	3	220
"	Sibelius	5	234
E major	Bruckner	7	102
E minor	Brahms	4	96
"	Dvořák	5	112
"	Hanson	1	126
"	Rachmaninoff	2	204
"	Sibelius	1	226
"	Tchaikovsky	5	252
F major	Beethoven	6	68
"	Beethoven	8	74
"	Brahms	3	94
F minor	Tchaikovsky	4	250
"	Vaughan Williams		260
F♯ minor	Haydn	45	154
G major	Dvořák	4	110
"	Haydn	6	142
"	Haydn	11	150
"	Hill	3	157
"	Mahler	4	167

INDEX ACCORDING TO KEYS

Index by Titles

SYMPHONY THEMES